MERCHANDISING MATHEMATICS

A MARKETING APPROACH

Andrea L. Weeks * Madelyn C. Perenchio * Veronica J. Miller

Edited by

Dorothy A. Metcalfe

All of The Fashion Institute of Design and Merchandising

Los Angeles

MERRILL PUBLISHING COMPANY

A Bell & Howell Information Company

Columbus * Toronto * London * Melbourne

Published by Merrill Publishing Company
A Bell & Howell Information Company
Columbus, Ohio 43216

This book was set in Palatino

Administrative Editor: John Stout
Production Coordinator: JoEllen Gohr
Cover Designer: Russ Maselli

Library of Congress Catalog Card Number: 89-60668
International Standard Book Number: 0-675-21065-8
Printed in the United States of America
1 2 3 4 5 6 7 8 9—93 92 91 90

Dedication

Merchandising Mathematics: A Marketing Approach is dedicated to the students and faculty of The Fashion Institute of Design and Merchandising for their patience and input while this book was being created, and to our families and friends who believed in us and made sacrifices that allowed us to complete the project.

Preface

The choice of a career in marketing, which encompasses the fields of buying, wholesaling, and manufacturing, is an affirmation of the desire to be involved with the world. Marketing is a universal tool by which needs and desires are fulfilled through producing, buying, and selling goods or services. However, to become successful in a marketing career, it is necessary to have a knowledge of some basic mathematics. *Mathematics is the controlling factor that allows a marketing strategy to be beneficial to the consumer, manufacturer, wholesaler, and retailer.* Mathematics is the *key* to marketing management and control. It is a planning and control device that allows the individual to develop objectives and, therefore, provides a concrete means of evaluating progress against the plan.

This book is divided into four parts: Basics, Pricing, Repricing and Inventory, and Profit. Each part contains chapters detailing information on these subjects that are so vital to success in the marketing world. Business concepts, chapter objectives, and key terms are explained in clear, concise language; formulas for computing problems are outlined step by step; finally, students are given sample and in-class problems with homework and special challengers to reinforce classroom learning. It is the objective of this book to provide readers with explanations and sufficient practice in order to develop their expertise in the basic concepts and mechanics of marketing and merchandising math, enabling them to acquire the basic knowledge needed to succeed in their chosen field of study.

Acknowledgments

This book would not have been possible without the invaluable support of many individuals. Therefore, we want to thank the following authors: Gary Armstrong, M. Wayne Delozier, James F. Engel, Newton E. Godnick, Thomas C. Kinnear, Philip Koltler, and Martin R. Warshaw.

In addition, we wish to extend our appreciation for the support provided by the following staff and faculty members of The Fashion Institute of Design and Merchandising: Sharon Charles, Viki Deyoe, Suzanna Grueser, Patrice Hughes, Dan Jaffee, Gail Jenkins, Bill Lee, Michael Lindley, Dr. Norma Melone, Jim Nemmert, Debbie Reiner, Charlotte Rose, Susan Roy, Les Sechler, Rick Trotta, and Gail Williamson

The following reviewers were immensely helpful in their suggestions and general input and we gratefully acknowledge their contributions: Stan Adamski, Owens Technical College; Holly Bastow-Shoop, Ph. D., North Dakota State University; Louis D. Canale, Ph. D., Genesee Community College; Bernice Dandridge, Solano Community College; Gary M. Donnelly, Casper College; Louis Frank, Jr., Dundalk Community College; Laura Jolley, Oklahoma State University; Judy Kraft, Northeast Wisconsin Technical College; Roy O. Kruger, Warner Pacific College; Frank McDaniels, Delaware County Community College; Jack Porter, West Virginia University; Rebecca Shidel, Georgia Institute of Technology; Elizabeth Taylor, Art Institute of Atlanta; and Judy L. Witt, Waukesha County Technical Institute.

We would like to thank the editors and staff of Merrill Publishing Company for their insight, guidance, and belief in this book.

Lastly, we are indebted to our students, who provided questions and feedback in the teaching of this complex subject.

CONTENTS

PART 1: BASICS

Chapter 1:   Word Problem Guidelines/Rules of Rounding   1
                Work Unit   3
                Summary and Key Terms   11

Chapter 2:   Review of Percentage and Percentage Increase/Decrease
                Concept   13
                Work Unit   14
                Summary and Key Terms   27

PART 2: PRICING

Chapter 3:   Pricing and Markup Concept   29
                Work Unit   32
                Summary and Key Terms   51

Chapter 4:   Markup of Groups Concept   53
                Work Unit   56
                Summary and Key Terms   88

Chapter 5:   Terms of the Sale Concept   89
                Work Unit   92
                Summary and Key Terms   107

Chapter 6:   Averaging of Markups Concept   109
                Work Unit   112
                Summary and Key Terms   148

Chapter 7:   Midterm Review
                Problems   149
                Solutions   164

PART 3: REPRICING AND INVENTORY

Chapter 8:   Repricing of Merchandise Concept   175
     Work Unit   180
     Summary and Key Terms   203

Chapter 9:   Closing Inventory Concept   205
     Work Unit   210
     Summary and Key Terms   223

PART 4: PROFIT

Chapter 10:   Skeletal Profit and Loss Concept   225
     Work Unit   227
     Summary and Key Terms   243

Chapter 11:   Detailed Profit and Loss Concept   245
     Work Unit   248
     Summary and Key Terms   278

Chapter 12:   Final Review
     Problems   279
     Solutions   300

PART ONE: BASICS

CHAPTER ONE
Word Problem Guidelines and Rules of Rounding

OBJECTIVES

After completing this chapter, you should be able to:

- Successfully read and comprehend word problems.
- Correctly round a number using three different methods.
- Express numbers in the proper form as related to common business practice.
- Apply the principles learned to a business situation.

CONCEPT

This unit deals with the two areas that most often present a challenge to the student—word problems and rounding numbers. Although these concepts are elementary, word problems and rounding are used daily in business. Therefore, a simple review is in order to make sure that everyone starts from the same base of knowledge.

The first area discussed in this unit is **word problem solving**. Word problems are important because they are a verbal expression of a mathematical question. In the work environment, your supervisor will rarely write out a question for you. More often than not, communication will be verbal; e.g., while you are out on the selling floor, your boss asks you what percent of the stock you sold. This is a word problem. Your ability to answer questions like this will depend on how well you solve word problems. Following the ten-step procedure in this chapter will help you:

1. Develop the ability to recognize key words;
2. Delete extraneous material; and
3. Use the proper formulas correctly.

Once you have developed sufficient facility with word problems, the next major challenge is expressing the correct answer in the accepted form. This process involves the procedure known as **rounding**.

The concept of rounding is simple: It is a procedure that allows you to express the number in shortened form. However, since the introduction of computers to the business world, there are now three common ways of rounding used that apply to different business situations. These three methods are:

1. Rounding by looking to the number to the immediate right of the digit to be rounded (e.g., 54.445 is rounded to 54.4);

2. Rounding by truncating, or cutting off, the number at a certain point regardless of what the rest of the number is (e.g. 54.445 is rounded to 54.4); and

3. Rounding by looking at the number to the farthest right and rounding forward (to the left) up to the digit required (e.g., 54.445 is rounded to 54.5).

The last method of rounding, from the far right, is most often used when a buyer or wholesaler is trying to determine markup or profit of merchandise. Therefore, this is the method we will use in this book. The main point to remember in this procedure is not to round too far. Express the number in its proper form (i.e., units are expressed as whole numbers, dollars are usually expressed to an even cent, and percents are expressed to the first decimal).

DEFINITIONS OF TERMS USED IN THIS CHAPTER

Rounding — a procedure that results in expressing a number in a shortened form.
Rounding—looking to the immediate right method — procedure that shortens the number by checking one decimal place beyond the required form.
Rounding—looking to the far right method — procedure that shortens the number by starting at the far right and rounding decimal by decimal to the required form.
Truncating method — procedure that shortens the number by "cutting off" the number at the required decimal.
Word problem — a verbal expression of a mathematical question.

FORMULA: THE STEPS IN SOLVING WORD PROBLEMS

If you are careful to follow these ten steps, you should have no trouble.

1. Read the entire problem through once.

2. Stay calm.

3. Read the entire program through a second time, listing how many and what types of answers are needed.

4. Cross out all unnecessary words (story words).

5. Do not cross out key words: any numbers, any marketing terms (e.g., sales, cost, plan, amount spent, etc.).

6. Write down all formulas that seem to apply to the problem.

7. Convert all words to the arithmetic functions indicated. For example:

of	bottom of the fraction
less	subtraction
missing	subtraction
was, is, are, were	equals (top of the fraction)

plan	total
increase	addition
more	addition
decrease	subtraction
has, have, had	equals

8. Arrange problem **chronologically** (by time sequence); for example, you buy first, next sell some, then adjust retail price, sell some more, etc.

9. Work the problem in the chronological order established—solving for the unknown in the first action, then moving on to the next time sequence. Circle each answer as you find it and identify it.

10. Make sure all your answers reflect what you are dealing with (i.e., units of items are expressed as whole numbers; dollars are rounded off to even cents; percents are rounded off to the first decimal point, or tenths).

SAMPLE PROBLEM

Mary Jane has 15 apples. She gives Bob 20.0% of them. She then gives Suzie 50.0% of what she has left. How many did she give to Bob? Suzie? How many does she have left for herself?

STEP 1:   Read the problem through once.

STEP 2:   Stay calm! Take a deep breath and get ready to read the problem again.

STEP 3:   Read the problem through once again and list how many and what types of answers will be required to solve the problem completely.

Mary Jane has 15 apples. She gives Bob 20.0% of them. She then gives Suzie 50.0% of what she has left. *How many did she give to Bob? Suzie? How many does she have left for herself?*

Answers needed:

A. How many apples did Mary give Bob?

B. How many apples did Mary Jane give to Suzie?

C. How many apples did Mary Jane have left for herself?

STEP 4:   Cross out all unnecessary words in the problem when you read the problem through for the third time.

Mary Jane has 15 ~~apples. She gives~~ Bob 20.0% of ~~them. She~~ then ~~gives~~ Suzie 50.0% of ~~what she has~~ left. *How many ~~did she give~~ to Bob? Suzie? How many ~~does she have~~ left for herself?*

STEP 5:   Arrange all the numbers in a chart or formula that applies to the situation.

number of apples given to Bob = x
number of apples given to Suzie = y
number of apples Mary Jane has left = 15 – x – y

$$\frac{\text{part}}{\text{whole}} = \% \text{ (key)}$$

Formula to find the number of apples given to Bob:

$$\frac{x}{15} = 20\%$$

Formula to find the number of apples given to Suzie:

$$\frac{y}{15 - x} = 50\%$$

Formula to find the number of apples left for Mary Jane:

$$15 - x - y = \text{number left}$$

STEP 6:   Convert all words that indicate arithmetic functions to the correct sign.

Mary Jane *has* (=) 15 ~~apples. She gives~~ Bob 20.0% *of* (bottom of fraction) ~~them.~~
~~She~~ then ~~gives~~ Suzie 50.0% *of* (bottom of fraction) ~~what she has~~ left. How many ~~did~~
~~she give~~ to Bob? Suzie ? How many ~~does she have~~ left ~~for herself?~~

STEP 7:   Arrange all actions chronologically.

A. Mary Jane has 15 apples.
B. She gives Bob 20.0% of them.
C. She gives Suzie 50.0% of what she has left.
D. She keeps the remainder.

STEP 8:   Work the problems in chronological order, solving for the unknown quantity in this
time sequence.

A. Mary Jane has 15 apples.

(There is nothing to solve here; it is merely a statement of fact.)

B. She gives Bob 20.0% of them (use formula established in Step 7).

$$\frac{x}{15} = 20\% \text{ (key)}$$

Multiply:

15×20 (% key) = 3

x = 3 (Bob was given 3 apples.)

C. She then gives Suzie 50.0% of what she has left (use formula established in Step 7).

$$\frac{y}{15 - x} = 50.0\%$$

or since x = 3 established earlier

$$\frac{y}{15 - 3} = 50.0\%$$

or
$$\frac{y}{12} = 50.0\%$$

Multiply:

12×50.0 (% key) = 6

y = 6 (Suzie was given 6 apples.)

D. Mary Jane keeps the rest (use formula established in Step 7).

$15 - x - y$ = number kept

x = 3
y = 6
$15 - 3 - 6 = 6$

Mary Jane keeps 6 apples for herself.

STEP 9:   Identify all answers.

Bob got 3 apples.

Suzie got 6 apples.

Mary Jane kept 6 apples.

STEP 10:   Make sure all answers required to solve the problems are expressed in the correct form.

Since we are discussing apples in this problem, the correct form would be whole units. All our answers are in whole units and are therefore correct.

RULES FOR ROUNDING NUMBERS

1. All units are expressed as whole numbers (e.g., 1, 762, 565).

2. Money is usually expressed as dollars and even cents (e.g., $15.35, $1,284.72).

3. All percentages are expressed to the first decimal place, or tenths (e.g., 51.4%, 68.3%).

4. To round off a number on a calculator, make sure your calculator is set on a floating decimal point so that it shows as many decimal places as possible.

5. Next, starting at the farthest number to the right, round off one decimal place at a time.

6. Continue the procedure using this rule:

   "If the number is 5 or greater, increase the next number to the left by one; if the number is 4 or less, leave it alone" until you have expressed the number in the terms stated in Rules 1, 2, and 3.

SAMPLE PROBLEMS

A. Round off the following number, which represents the units of stock planned as an increase of the sweater inventory in the Newcastle store: 576.85369.

STEP 1:   Determine the form in which the number should be expressed.

              Units = a whole number

STEP 2:   Start at the number to the extreme right and round using our "5 or greater rule = up one; 4 or less = leave alone."

              Substep a.   576.85369
              Substep b.   9 is greater than 5, so increase the next decimal to the left
                             and drop the 9.
              Result*: c.   576.8537

              *Answer is not yet expressed as a whole unit.

STEP 3:   Repeat the procedure using the new number.

              Substep a.   576.8537
              Substep b.   7 is greater than 5, so increase the next decimal to the left
                             and drop the 7.
              Result*: c.   576.854

              *Answer is not yet expressed as a whole unit.

STEP 4: Repeat the procedure.

Substep a. 576.85<u>4</u>
Substep b. 4 is less than 5, so leave the next decimal place to the left
alone and drop the 4.
Result*: c. 576.85

*Answer is not yet expressed as a whole unit.

STEP 5: Repeat the procedure.

Substep a. 576.85
Substep b. 5 is equal to 5, so increase the next decimal place to the left
and drop the 5.
Result*: c. 576.9

*Answer is not yet expressed as a whole unit.

STEP 6: Repeat the procedure.

Substep a. 576.9
Substep b. 9 is greater than 5, so increase the next decimal to the left
and drop the 9.
Result*: c. 577

*Answer is now expressed as a whole unit.

B. What is the correct rounded percentage of markup if your calculator reads 61.5796431%?

STEP 1: Percentages are expressed to the first decimal place.

STEP 2: Start at the number to the right and round according to the rule.

Substep a. 61.5796431%
Substep b. 1 is less than 5, so leave the next decimal place alone and
drop the 1.
Result*: c. 61.579643%

*Answer is not yet expressed as a rounded percentage.

STEP 3:   Repeat the procedure.

                Substep   a.   61.579643%
                Substep   b.   3 is less than 5, so leave the next decimal place alone and drop
                               the 3.
                Result*: c.   61.57964%

                *Answer is not yet expressed as a rounded percentage.

STEP 4:   Repeat the procedure.

                Substep   a.   61.57964%
                Substep   b.   4 is less than 5, so leave the next decimal place alone and drop
                               the 4.
                Result*: c.   61.5796%

                *Answer is not yet expressed as a rounded percentage.

STEP 5:   Repeat the procedure.

                Substep   a.   61.5796%
                Substep   b.   6 is greater than 5, so increase the next decimal place and drop
                               the 6.
                Result*: c.   61.580%

                *Answer is not expressed as a rounded percentage.

STEP 6:   Repeat the procedure.

                Substep   a.   61.580%
                Substep   b.   0 is less than 5, so leave the next decimal alone and drop
                               the 0.
                Result*: c.   61.58%

                *Answer is not expressed as a rounded percentage.

STEP 7:   Repeat the procedure.

                Substep   a.   61.58%
                Substep   b.   8 is greater than 5, so increase the next decimal place and drop
                               the 8.
                Result*: c.   61.6%

                *Answer is expressed to first decimal place.

IN-CLASS PRACTICE PROBLEMS

1. Round off to whole numbers.

   a. 653.459 _____

   b. 75.65454 _____

   c. 6.44445 _____

   d. 66677.2345 _____

2. Round off the following percentages to the correct decimal.

   a. 60.00023% _____

   b. 152.54546% _____

   c. 62.44445% _____

   d. 71.4743% _____

3. Round off the following dollar amounts to the correct cents.

   a. $61.43217 _____

   b. $81.4546 _____

   c. $151,562.04679 _____

HOMEWORK

1. Round off the following numbers to whole numbers, percentages, and dollars.

	Whole #'s	Percentages	$
a. 64.321469	_____	_____	_____
b. 81.9432	_____	_____	_____
c. 1645.7326	_____	_____	_____
d. 581.9243	_____	_____	_____

2. A manufacturer looks at her calculator and sees the numbers $443.7496. If she is looking for the dollar price for a food processor, what is the correct price?

3. A divisional merchandise manager looks at her buyer's purchase order and sees the markup percentage written as 51.445%. What is the correct percentage?

4. A store manager is told to transfer 63.4% of his spark plugs to a new store. Since he has 1,046 units of spark plugs, his calculator shows he must transfer 663.164 units. Exactly how many spark plugs should he transfer?

CHALLENGER

A buyer must transfer 66 dresses from her stock of 862 units. What is the percentage of stock she is transferring?

CHAPTER ONE: SUMMARY

The use of verbal communication has historically been a keystone to all business transactions. However, it is critical in today's world of computerized, instantaneous transmission that accuracy and precision must provide the direction for business information exchange. Only by establishing common ground rules can we avoid making costly mistakes.

KEY TERMS

Rounding
Rounding—looking to the immediate right method
Rounding—looking to the far right method
Truncating Method
Word Problems

CHAPTER TWO
Review of Percentage and Percentage Increase/Decrease

OBJECTIVES

After completing this chapter, you should be able to:

- Identify a percentage problem.
- Utilize the basic percentage formula.
- Identify the basic percentage increase/decrease factors.
- Recognize appropriate formulas needed in percentage increase/decrease problems.

CONCEPT

Percentage is one of the most commonly used concepts in business. A percentage expresses the relationship of the size of one number to the size of another number (part to whole). By talking in percentages, the business person can more accurately describe the current situation. For example, if you were to state that you sold 15 towels yesterday, we would not know if the performance were good or bad unless we knew how many you usually sell, how many you were expected to sell, how many you received, and how many you have left. However, if you were to say you sold 15 towels, which was a 30.0% increase over the day before, or you sold 15 towels today, which was 75.0% of what you received (sell-through), then we would have a more accurate assessment of your business trend. Percentage allows you to compare one number to another to give:

1. measure of progress;
2. measure of improvement; and
3. measure of size.

The key to being successful with percentage is to identify which is the part and which is the whole. The part is the number that is being compared to another number.

Percentage increase/decrease is a specialized usage of the percentage formula. In its own way, this concept is easier than percentage because there is never a question as to which is the part. The whole is immediately identified as the original number (the one that occurred first). Therefore, using the standard formula and the percent key, you can use percentage increase/decrease to show improvement.

Facility with the percentage formula is essential to your success in business. Since it is the most commonly used mathematical concept in the work environment, your career can actually depend on how well you are able to identify the part and the whole and calculate the answer.

DEFINITIONS OF TERMS USED IN THIS CHAPTER

Dollar difference — the amount added to (increase) or subtracted from (decrease) the original amount. This is part of the original amount.
Increase/decrease — the difference between the original amount and the new amount.
New amount — the number which occurred second in time. This is **not** part of the original amount.
Original amount — the number that occurred first and to which the new amount is being compared.
Percentage — the relationship between a part and whole expressed as part of 100.

PERCENT FORMULA

$$\frac{\text{part}}{\text{whole}} = \% \text{ (key)}$$

SAMPLE PROBLEM

A. A buyer's sales in her department this week were $500.00. She did 25.0% of her entire department's business in the blouse classification. What were her sales in blouses this week?

STEP 1:   Formula:

$$\frac{\text{part}}{\text{whole}} = \% \text{ (key)}$$

Department sales = whole = $500.00
Blouse classification = part = x
Blouse % = part % = 25%

STEP 2:   Apply numbers to formula.

$$\frac{x}{500} = 25.0\% \text{ (key)}$$

STEP 3:   Multiply to get:

$500 \times 25.0 \text{ (\% key)} = \$125$

STEP 4:   Blouse sales = $125.00

STEP 5:   Recheck.

$125 \div 500 \text{ (\% key)} = 25.0\%$

IN-CLASS PRACTICE PROBLEMS

1. A videotape company's sales last year in October were $250,000.00. While analyzing the business, the owner discovered that comedies contributed 60% of this total. What were the sales in comedies last year?

2. The Missy sportswear buyer plans this year to buy 30.0% of last year's purchases, which were $100,000. What are this year's purchases?

3. The scarf sales amount to $50,000.00. This classification is part of the accessories division, which sells $900,000.00 worth of merchandise per year. What percentage is the scarf classification to the total accessories division?

4. Last week, you received 240 units of a food processor and sold 30 units. You are now analyzing your selling percentage to determine whether to reorder or not. What percent did you sell? Your standard strategy is to reorder if you sell 20.0% of any item within one week. Should you reorder this item?

5. A men's furnishings manufacturer's top line is underwear, which produces $20,000.00. This is 15.0% of the total sales. What is the dollar amount of the company's sales this year?

6. 100 is what percent of 30?

7. On May 1, your stock totals 136 pieces. During the month, you sold 1/5 of your stock. What percentage did you sell?

8. You sold 1/10 of your stock, which totaled 197 pieces. How many pieces and what percentage did you sell?

9. You received 40 units of a sweater. You sell 25.0%. How many units did you sell?

10. If you owe the government 17.0% of your profits and you pay $6,945.00, how much was your profit?

11. If you transfer 18.0% of your shirt stock each week, and transferred 7 units this week, how many shirts did you have at the beginning of the week?

12. Sixty-four percent (64%) of your lamps are table models. If your dollar inventory in lamps is $100,000.00, what is the dollar value of your table lamps?

13. You have 21 dozen sweaters to distribute evenly among your 14 branch stores. What percentage should each store receive?

14. A manufacturer of coats has 2,000 parkas that he hopes will sell out completely, providing 61.3% of his total company's sales. What are the total units planned to sell for his company?

PERCENTAGE INCREASE/DECREASE FORMULA

$\dfrac{\text{part}}{\text{whole}}$ = % key or $\dfrac{\text{difference}}{\text{original amount}}$ = % increase/decrease

new amount **+ or –** difference = original amount

original amount **+ or –** difference = new amount

new amount – original amount = difference

SAMPLE PROBLEM

A manufacturer sold 300 pairs of socks last year during the spring sale. This year, the same manufacturer sold 275 pairs. What is the percent of increase/decrease?

STEP 1:   *Formula:*

               new amount – original amount = difference

STEP 2:   Apply numbers to the formula.

               275 – 300 = –25

STEP 3:   Difference = 25 units less than last year.

STEP 4:   *Formula:*

               $\dfrac{\text{part}}{\text{whole}}$ = % key   or $\dfrac{\text{difference}}{\text{original amount}}$ = % increase/decrease (key)

STEP 5:   Apply numbers to the formula.

               $\dfrac{-25}{300}$ = x% (key)

STEP 6:   Divide to get:

   −25 ÷ 300 (% key) = −8.3%

STEP 7:   Percent decrease: −8.3%

STEP 8:   Recheck.

   8.3 × 300 (% key) = 25

IN-CLASS PRACTICE PROBLEMS

1. The baby department has 30.0% of its stock dollars placed in the layette classification. If the total stock is $300,000.00, what is the total dollar stock in the layette classification?

2. This year's sales for the Carroll's Trucking Company were $150,000.00 versus last year's sales of $ 100,000.00. What is this year's percent increase/decrease? dollar increase/decrease?

3. DeNike's Supermarket has a 60.0% increase this year versus last year's sales of $200,000.00. What is the dollar increase? What is this year's sales in dollars?

4. A pillow manufacturer sold 2,000 units in July last year. This year she plans to sell 3,500 units. What is the projected percent increase?

5. The housewares buyer plans to buy 21.3% more plastic glasses this year. Last year, he bought $150,000.00 in this classification. What is his open-to-buy plan in this class this year?

SPECIAL PERCENT INCREASE/DECREASE FORMULA

$$\frac{\text{new amount}}{\text{original amount}} = \frac{\begin{array}{c}100\% + \text{increase (\% key)}\\ \text{OR}\\ 100\% - \text{decrease (\%key)}\end{array}}{}$$

SAMPLE PROBLEM

This month, the case goods buyer's sales were $250,000, which was a 36.0% increase over last month's sales. What were last month's sales dollars?

STEP 1:   Establish the relationship between last month's and this month's sales. Since this month shows an increase over last month, we add the percent increase to 100% (% + 100% = % increase).

STEP 2:   Apply numbers to the formula.

                 100% + 36.0% = 136.0%

STEP 3:   Formula:

$$\frac{\text{new amount}}{\text{original amount}} = \frac{\begin{array}{c}100\% + \text{increase (\% key)}\\ \text{OR}\\ 100\% - \text{decrease (\%key)}\end{array}}{}$$

STEP 4:   Apply numbers to the formula.

$$\frac{250,000}{x} = 136.0 \ (\% \ key)$$

STEP 5:   Divide to get:

$250,000 \div 136\% = \$183,823.52$

STEP 6:   Last month's sales = $183,823.52

STEP 7:   Recheck.

$$\frac{250,000}{183,823.52} = 136 \ (\% \ key)$$

$136 \times 183,823.52 \ (\% \ key) = 250,000$

IN-CLASS PRACTICE PROBLEMS

1. In doing her six-month plan, Mary Jones sees that her active-wear classification is trending 60.0% ahead of last year. In accordance with this trend, she plans this year's August sales at $60,000.00. What were last year's sales in August?

2. This year, the Magic Handbag Company plans a 30.0% increase in business. This year's sales plan is $300,000.00. What were last year's sales?

3. This year, the bath and bedding buyer plans her bath accessories to have a 23.1% decrease. Therefore, this year's sales plan is $300,000.00. What did she do in this classification last year?

4. The produce department did $70,000.00 in April, which was 8.3% increase over last year's sales. What were last year's sales?

5. The divisional merchandise manager for ready-to-wear makes out her advertising budget and is informed by upper management that she must plan a 20.0% decrease from last year. This leaves her with $112, 000.00 to spend on advertising in December. What was last year's budget in December? What was the dollar difference?

6. A table linens manufacturer plans to have a 7.6% decrease this year. This year's sales are planned at $540,000.00. What were last year's sales? What is the dollar difference?

HOMEWORK

1. The home-store manager has 200 sets of Lemon china in her department. This represents 30.0% of the stock units in the china department. How many units are in this department?

2. In the Downtown store, the athletic-shoe division has sales of $500,000.00. In the Essex store, the same division does 85.0% of the sales produced in the downtown store. What are the dollar sales in the athletic-shoe division for the Essex store?

3. A rug manufacturer owns 130 Persian rugs, which is 20.0% of his total inventory. What is the current inventory in units?

4. The Jones Auto Parts Store's dollar increase this year was $25,000.00. This was a 9.0% increase over last year. What were last year's sales?

5. The bathing suit manager sent 10.8% of her bikini stock and 12.0% of her bandeau stock to the downtown store. Her total bandeau stock was $2,480.00 while her bikini stock was $3,860.00. What was the dollar amount of the transfer?

6. A sales representative whose commission rate is 3.0% of his total sales earned $85.00 in commissions this month. What were his total sales?

7. A wholesaler sells 800 units of socks this month, which represents a 35% increase over last month. What were the units sold last month?

8. Last month's sales were $50,000.00 higher than this month's sales. This was a 14.3% decrease. What were last month's sales? This month's sales?

CHALLENGERS

1. A buyer of a downtown store has an inventory of $5,000.00 on hand in February. On March 1, she claimed the following merchandise:

   76 scarves at $3.75 each
   138 barrettes at $1.75 each
   51 silk flowers at $2.75 each
   10 sunglasses at $15.00 each

   What percentage of her inventory was claimed at $3.75? $1.75? $2.75? $15.00? What percentage did each price point contribute dollarwise to the total claim?

2. A tire manufacturer has a 32.6% increase this year over last year's sales of $93,000.00. Last year's sales were 7.6% greater than the year before. What is this year's sales? Last year's dollar increase over two year's ago? This year's dollar increase? The dollar sales for two years ago? What is the dollar and percent increase this year compared to two years ago?

CHAPTER TWO: SUMMARY

Percentage is the most important means of communication in the business world. Only by comparing the size of one number to another can we express progress or improvement. Facility with percentage is essential to success in a marketing career.

KEY TERMS

Dollar difference
Increase/decrease
New amount
Original amount
Percentage

PART TWO: PRICING

CHAPTER THREE
Pricing and Markup

OBJECTIVES

After completing this chapter, you should be able to:

- Identify and understand the four pricing factors.
- Identify a basic markup problem.
- Understand how markup percent relates to profit.
- Utilize and apply the markup percent (%) and markup percent complement formulas.

CONCEPT

The art of pricing is a vital part of any successful marketing strategy. The marketing manager faced with the challenge of finding the "right price" must consider the following factors:

1. cost;
2. retail reductions;
3. overhead expenses;
4. profit margin;
5. customer acceptance.

The combination of these five factors helps the marketing manager determine the selling price of the goods. The first four factors are mathematical in nature and determine the ideal price from the company's point of view. The fifth factor—customer acceptance—tells the marketing manager if the company's ideal price represents a value to the target market.

Since the first four factors (cost, retail reductions, overhead, and profit margin) must be included in the selling price of the merchandise, each of these factors must be analyzed in detail.

Cost of the merchandise is the first factor to be considered. The cost of the merchandise refers to the amount the company pays the supplier for the merchandise. To make money and stay in business, the marketing manager must charge a higher price than the amount of money paid for the merchandise.

The second factor to consider is **retail reductions**. Retail reductions are composed of **markdowns, employee discount, and shortage. Markdown** is the procedure in which the selling price has been lowered to a new, more saleable level. The causes and reasons for markdowns will be covered later in this book, but the key right now is their effect on profit: markdowns lower profitability. Therefore, since markdowns have an adverse effect on profit, the loss must be made up. On all merchandise, a certain amount of the selling price is devoted to the offset of markdowns in the total merchandise group.

Another component of retail reductions to consider is *employee discount*. Employee discount is a benefit to employees of the company in which the selling price is lowered as an incentive for them to buy and use the merchandise. The net effect is the same as markdown in that the profit is adversely affected. As in markdown, this loss from the employee discount must be analyzed and planned as part of the selling price of the merchandise.

The third component of retail reduction to consider is shortage. Shortage is the loss of inventory due to bookkeeping errors or theft. Because this merchandise was not sold or was charged to the department incorrectly, shortage has an adverse effect on profit. Like markdowns and employee discount, this loss must be considered, estimated, and included as part of the selling price.

When markdowns, employee discount, and shortage have all been estimated, the marketing manager totals them together to derive the retail reduction number. This number is then added to the cost of the merchandise as the second step in deriving the "right" selling price for the company.

The third factor to be considered is *overhead* expenses. Overhead expenses are the daily cost of doing business. These expenses include personnel, building maintenance, advertising, administrative costs and expenses. Once the overhead expenses are estimated, this number is in turn added to the cost and retail reductions as the third step involved in determining the selling price.

The last factor involved in the mathematical determination of the selling price is the *profit margin*. A profit margin is essential to the health of any business. Profit provides the money necessary to expand the business and to provide dividends to the investors. It is important to know that a certain profit margin must be added into the price of every item handled. Once the profit margin is estimated, it too is added to the cost, retail reductions, and overhead to derive the selling price.

Utilizing mathematics, the marketing manager now has derived the selling price that is right for the company. However, is this price the "right" price for the customer? Not necessarily!

Merchandise marketing is an art as well as a science. Mathematics can tell the merchant what selling price to put on the merchandise to make a profit. However, if the price is so high that the customer will not buy the item, then the marketing manager still has made no money. The science of mathematics must be tempered by the marketing manager's knowledge of the customer.

Naturally, this is the most difficult part of pricing because the marketing manager is trying to predict something that is unpredictable—people. However, by using demographic studies, developing psychographic profiles, and studying past performances of other items, the marketing manager can estimate whether the customer will perceive the price to be appropriate.

As you can see, this process is fairly involved. To simplify the procedure, the market manager does just *one analysis* of cost, retail reductions, overheads, and profit margin for the year and uses this study to determine the markup goal for all of the merchandise. Then he or she only has to assess each item bought by using a mathematical formula and ask whether the customer will pay the price. If the answer is yes, the marketing manager goes ahead; if the answer is no, he or she must think of an alternative—either not buy the item or find a a substitute that will provide the needed markup.

The process of markup (cost plus retail reductions plus overhead plus profit) *is the factor that determines the success or failure of a business.* Because markup is so important, it is planned and checked periodically to make sure the goal is being achieved.

The control process can be exceedingly cumbersome, especially when dealing with large quantities of merchandise. Therefore, the easiest way to handle the problem is to watch the *markup percent.* Markup percent is the relationship of the markup dollars (the money to cover retail reductions, overhead, and profit) compared to the selling price. By using markup dollars as the **part** and the selling price (retail) as the **whole**, merchants can tell what percent of sales covers the expenses and profit. Furthermore, by knowing how much of the retail is markup dollars, the marketing manager can keep track of how much money is being spent on the cost of the merchandise. This would be important to make sure the best deal possible is gotten from the suppliers.

Knowing that markup dollars and cost are the two parts that make up the whole (retail) means that whenever you know two of these elements, you can find the other. Cost and markup dollars are **complements** of each other, a part that, when added to another part, makes a whole.

The process of markup is followed regardless of the type of buying that is being performed.

INTERNATIONAL BUYING

In the case of international buying, there is more than one cost to be considered. When merchandise is purchased, the cost of the item is figured based on the current exchange rate. This is called the **first cost.** However, upon arrival, the cost of freight and duties charged must be added to the item. This is called the **landed cost.** From this point, the procedure of markup is the same. Marketing manager takes the landed cost and the markup percent goal and calculates the selling price. Often because there is greater risk in international buying (goods generally cannot be returned to the vendor if defective) and because of the exclusive nature of the merchandise, a larger profit margin will be figured into the selling price to cover the risks. However, the procedure of pricing is the same in spite of the fact that the merchandise has been imported.

SPECIFICATION BUYING

The purchase of **specification (private-label) goods** is also another specialized form of buying. In this case, the private-label goods have the store name as the brand name. This merchandise is exclusively the property of the store. It is made to suit the needs of the store's target customer. However, even though this merchandise is exclusive to the store, the procedure of markup is the same.

Markup and pricing are essential to the success of the business. Markup creates the income for the company. The company stays healthy and grows if the selling price is mathematically calculated taking into consideration all of the factors and tempered through the use of customer profiles.

DEFINITIONS OF TERMS USED IN THIS UNIT

Complement — a part of the whole that, when added to the other part, makes a complete item.
Cost — the actual price charged by the manufacturer and paid by the buyer for the merchandise purchased.
Markup dollars — the money the buyer adds to the cost of the merchandise to create the retail price.
Markup percent — The relationship between the markup dollars and the retail price expressed as part of 100.
Retail — the price the buyer charges the ultimate consumer for the merchandise.

FORMULAS

Cost + markup dollars = retail
Retail – cost = markup dollars
Retail – markup dollars = cost

SAMPLE PROBLEMS

A. A buyer pays $16.00 for a blouse and adds markup dollars of $20.00. What is the retail price?

STEP 1:   Formula:

cost + markup dollars = retail

STEP 2:   Apply the numbers to the equation.

$16.00 + $20.00 = $36.00

RESULT: Retail = $36.00

B. A buyer pays $10.00 cost for an item and determines that the retail should be $17.50. What is the amount of the markup?

STEP 1:   Formula:

retail − cost = markup dollars

STEP 2:   Apply the numbers to the equation.

$17.50 − $10.00 = $7.50

RESULT: Markup dollars = $7.50

****

BASIC MARKUP RULE #1:

When figuring pricing factors for a single unit of merchandise, always figure the cost per unit in a problem that lists a cost based on multiple units.

****

IN-CLASS PRACTICE PROBLEMS

1. Fill in the following chart.

Cost	Retail	Markup $
$ 25.00	$ 55.00	
	$ 27.50	$ 22.50
$573.00	$ 862.99	
	$1,110.00	$867.50
$ 18.85		$ 15.36
$ 33.00		$ 29.00

2. A general merchandise manager knows that the retail of a coat is $275.00 and the markup dollars are $125.00. What is the cost?

3. A buyer purchases a style of jeans that costs $164.00 per dozen and adds markup dollars of $14.00 each. What is the retail (*Hint: figure cost per unit first*)?

4. A rug manufacturer charges $28.50 cost for a small area rug. Suggested retail is $65.00. What are the suggested markup dollars?

MARKUP PERCENT FORMULA WHEN MARKUP DOLLARS ARE KNOWN

$$\frac{part}{whole} = (\% \text{ key}) \quad \text{or} \quad \frac{markup \$}{retail} = (\% \text{ key})$$

SAMPLE PROBLEM

A buyer pays $30.00 cost and adds $35.00 more in markup dollars. What is the retail? What is the markup percent?

STEP 1:   Formula:

cost + markup $ = retail

STEP 2:   Apply numbers to the formula.

$30.00 + $35.00 = $65.00

STEP 3:   Retail = $65.00

STEP 4:   Formula:

$$\frac{\text{markup \$}}{\text{retail}} = \text{markup (\% key)}$$

STEP 5:   Apply numbers to the equation.

$$\frac{\$35.00}{\$65.00} = x\%$$

STEP 6:   Divide to get:

$35.00 ÷ $65.00 (% key) = 53.84615%

RESULT: Markup % = 53.9%

FORMULA WHEN ONLY COST AND RETAIL ARE KNOWN

$$\frac{\text{retail} - \text{cost}}{\text{retail}} \text{ or } \frac{\text{markup \$}}{\text{retail}} = \text{markup \% (key)}$$

SAMPLE PROBLEM

A buyer pays $13.00 cost for a skirt and retails it for $31.50. What is the markup percent?

STEP 1:   Formula:

retail − cost = markup $

STEP 2:   Apply numbers to formula.

$31.50 − $13.00 = $18.50

STEP 3:   Markup $ = $18.50

STEP 4:   Formula:

$$\frac{\text{markup \$}}{\text{retail}} = \text{markup \% (key)}$$

STEP 5:   Apply numbers to the formula.

$$\frac{\$18.50}{\$31.50} = x\% \text{ (key)}$$

STEP 6:   Divide to get:

$18.50 ÷ $31.50 (% key) = 58.73015%

RESULT: Markup % = 58.7%

IN-CLASS PRACTICE PROBLEMS

1. Fill in the following chart.

Cost	Retail	Markup $	Markup %
$ 6.00	$ 12.50		
$ 19.55	$ 38.79		
$350.00		$ 72.00	
$ 22.50/dz*	$ 5.50		
$ 68.00	$329.00		
$ 75.00/dz*		$ 25.00/unit	
	$119.95	$ 37.09	

*Always figure cost per unit first in a problem that lists a cost based on multiple units.

2. A manager receives skirts that cost $35.00 each. What would be her markup percent if she retails them for $68.00?

3. A buyer purchases the following items: 500 jackets costing $14.00 to sell at $32.00 each; 700 slacks costing $15.00 each to retail at $27.00; and 60 sweaters costings $16.00 each to sell at $45.00. What is the markup percent of the jackets? the slacks? the sweaters? What are the markup dollars for each of the items purchased?

4. A wholesaler offers three styles of wall tapestries each costing $18.75 and suggests $21.35 as markup dollars. What is the suggested retail of the wall tapestries? the markup percent?

HOMEWORK

1. Fill in the following chart.

Cost	Retail	Markup $	Markup %
$ 15.50	$38.00		
$ 17.50	$78.00		
$ 28.00	$48.00		
$ 10.90	$50.00		
$ 11.00		$ 17.75	
$ 10.00		$ 18.00	
$ 6.50		$ 17.25	
$ 1,167.85		$ 2,832.15	
	$ 9.99	$ 5.84	
	$ 5.99	$ 4.93	
	$10.50	$ 6.63	
	$41.50	$ 22.63	

2. A buyer purchases a handbag that costs $63.00 and retails it for $138.00. What are her markup dollars and her markup percent?

3. A drugstore prescription costs $16.00 and has suggested markup dollars of $38.00. What is the suggested retail and markup percent?

4. A hardware manager compares a hedge trimmer that is retailed at $38.00 to another hedge trimmer that retails for $50.00. For the first item, the cost is $16.00 and the second has markup dollars of $35.00. What are the markup percents for item #1 and #2? What is the percentage difference?

FORMULA FOR FINDING RETAIL WHEN MARKUP DOLLARS PERCENT ARE KNOWN

$$\frac{\text{markup } \$}{\text{retail}} = \text{markup \% (key)}$$

SAMPLE PROBLEM

A buyer purchases a skirt and adds $25.00 in markup dollars, which gives her a 52.3% markup. What is the retail? cost?

STEP 1:   Basic markup % formula:

$$\frac{\text{markup } \$}{\text{retail}} = \text{markup \% (key)}$$

STEP 2:   Apply numbers to the formula.

$$\frac{\$25.00}{x} = 52.3\%$$

STEP 3:   Divide to get:

$25.00 \div 52.3$ (% key) = $47.801

STEP 4:   Retail = $47.80

STEP 5:   Formula for finding cost when retail and markup dollars are known:

Retail – markup $ = cost

STEP 6:   Apply numbers to the formula.

$47.80 – $625.00 = $22.80

STEP 7:   Cost = $22.80

STEP 8:   Recheck.

$$\frac{\$25.00}{\$47.80} = 52.3 \ (\% \ \text{key})$$

$$52.3\% \times \$47.80 = \$25.00$$

IN-CLASS PRACTICE PROBLEMS

1. Fill in the following chart.

Cost	Retail	Markup $	Markup %
		$18.00	54.3%
		$30.00	68.7%
$25.00		$50.00	
$15.00	$55.00		
	$16.75	$10.50	
		$43.00	63.4%
		$59.00	55.8%

2. A buyer purchases a blouse that she marks up 52.6%, getting $5.00 in markup dollars. What is the retail? cost?

3. A cosmetics manufacturer offers two products: a cleansing milk that she has marked up $15.00, giving a 51.3% markup, and a remoisturizing cream, that includes $65.00 in markup dollars, giving a 54.8% markup. What are the retails and costs for each item?

FINDING THE COST WHEN RETAIL AND MARKUP PERCENT ARE KNOWN

$$\frac{\text{Markup \$}}{\text{Retail}} = \text{Markup \% (key)}$$

SAMPLE PROBLEM

A car rental company offers a daily rental service that retails at $28.00 a day, providing a 51.7% markup. What are the cost and markup dollars for this service?

STEP 1:   Formula:

$$\frac{\text{markup \$}}{\text{retail}} = \text{markup \% (key)}$$

STEP 2:   Apply numbers to the formula.

$$\frac{x}{\$28.00} = 51.7 \ (\% \ \text{key})$$

STEP 3:   Multiply to get:

$28.00 \times 51.7 \ (\% \ \text{key}) = \$14.476$

STEP 4:   Markup $ = $14.48

STEP 5:   Formula to find cost:

retail − markup $ = cost

STEP 6:   Apply numbers to formula.

$28.00 − $14.48 = $13.52

STEP 7:   Cost = $13.52

STEP 8:   Recheck.

$$\frac{\$14.48}{\$28.00} = 51.7 \ (\% \ \text{key})$$

$14. 48 ÷ 51.7 (% key) = $28.00

IN-CLASS PRACTICE PROBLEMS

1. Fill in the following chart.

Cost	Retail	Markup $	Markup %
	$150.00		50.0%
	$185.00		60.0%
	$ 83.00		56.8%
	$ 5.69		48.3%
	$ 12.50		60.3%
	$ 15.00		54.3%

2. Using the departmental markups listed below, find the cost of an item that retails for $15.00.

    Hosiery — 53.6%; Housewares — 47.8%
    Accessories — 56.4%; Lamps — 49.8%

3. A Divisional Merchandise Manager wants to know the cost of an air conditioner her buyer purchased. She knows the departmental markup is 42.8% and the retail for the air conditioner is $185.00. What are the cost and the markup dollars?

4. The suggested retails of badminton sets vary for the spring line. The racket set is $24.99, the net-included model is $34.99, and the deluxe set is $49.99. The resulting markups are: 51.8% on the racket set, 52.7% on the net-included set, and 53.6% on the deluxe set. What are the cost and markup dollars on each set?

FINDING THE RETAIL WHEN COST AND MARKUP PERCENT ARE ONLY KNOWN FACTORS

100% − markup % = markup % complement

$$\frac{cost}{retail} = \text{markup \% complement (\% key)}$$

****
BASIC MARKUP % RULE #2:

When cost and markup percent are the only known price factors in a problem, you must use the markup percent complement formula to solve the problem.
****

SAMPLE PROBLEM

A buyer for the children's department pays $16.00 per dozen for plastic pants and gets 52.3% markup. What are the retail and markup dollars?

STEP 1: Find the cost per unit.

$16.00 ÷ 12 = $1.333

STEP 2: Cost per unit = $1.33.

STEP 3: Cost and markup percent only are known; therefore, you must use the complement formula.

STEP 4:   Find the markup percent complement.

                 100% − markup % = markup % complement

STEP 5:   Apply numbers to the formula.

                 100% − 52.3% = 47.7%

STEP 6:   Markup % complement formula:

                 $\dfrac{\text{cost}}{\text{retail}}$ = markup % complement (key)

STEP 7:   Apply numbers to the formula.

                 $\dfrac{\$1.33}{\text{x}}$ = 47.7 (% key)

STEP 8:   Divide to get:

                 $1.33 ÷ 47.7 (% key) =$2.788

STEP 9:   Retail = $2.79

STEP 10:   Recheck.

                 $\dfrac{\$1.33}{\$2.79}$ = 47.7% (key)

                 $1.33 ÷ $2.79 (% key) = 47.7%

STEP 11:   Markup dollars formula:

                 retail − cost = markup $

STEP 12:   Apply numbers to the formula.

                 $2.79 − $1.33 = $1.46

STEP 13:   Markup $ = $1.46

STEP 14:   Recheck.

                 $\dfrac{\$1.46}{\$2.79}$ = 52.3 (% key)

                 $1.46 ÷ 2.79 (% key) = 52.3%

IN-CLASS PRACTICE PROBLEMS

1. Fill in the following table.

Cost	Retail	Markup $	Markup %
$ 180.00/dz			60.0%
$ 36.00			61.4%
$ 28.00			58.6%
$ 38.00			47.6%
$ 55.00			59.3%
$ 60.00			51.4%
$ 398.00			53.2%
$ 400.00			59.8%

2. The hosiery buyer paid $50.00 per dozen for cashmere socks. If her markup was 51.6%, what was her retail?

3. A beauty salon has a cost of $16.95 for a set of acrylic nails. The salon needs a 51.3% markup on this service. What would be the retail price? The competition offers crystal nails at $20.00 cost and retails the service at $45.00. What is the markup percent for crystal nails?

4. The book buyer purchases some cookbooks at $165.00/dozen and sells them at a 49.9% markup. What are the retail and markup dollars?

5. A women's sportswear manufacturer offers bikinis, which cost $130.00 per half dozen. If the markup percent is 53.4%, what are the retail and markup dollars?

6. The dress shirt buyer purchases plaid oxford button-downs for $108.00 per dozen and gets a 56.7% markup. What are the retail and markup dollars?

HOMEWORK

1. Fill in the following chart.

Cost	Retail	Markup $	Markup %
$14.00			36.0%
$ 7.50	$18.00		
	$24.00		49.0%
$ 4.00			53.0%
	$ 9.00		61.0%
$13.50			48.0%
$ 9.75			60.0%
		$16.00	43.0%
		$46.70	63.0%
		$76.99	25.8%

2. A buyer pays for merchandise that costs $63.00 per dozen. She plans to take a 63.4% markup on the merchandise. What are her retail and markup dollars?

3. A buyer imports an artificial Christmas tree at $12.50 cost. She plans a 76.4% markup. What are her retail and markup dollars?

4. A buyer adds markup dollars of $53.00 per unit, planning to take a 54.8% markup. What are her cost and retail?

5. Fill in the following chart.

Cost	Retail	Markup $	Markup %
	$ 75.00		35.0%
	$ 37.00		50.0%
	$ 25.00		43.0%
	$ 30.00		19.1%
	$ 15.00		50.0%
	$ 17.00		52.1%
	$ 37.50	$ 14.97	
	$ 53.67	$ 14.92	
	$ 100.00	$ 76.80	
	$ 1,478.00	$ 568.00	
	$ 436.00	$ 342.78	
	$23,456.78	$12,345.67	

6. A manager retails an item at $789.00 and takes a markup of 56.9%. What are the cost and markup dollars?

7. A buyer has an item in her stock with a retail of $123.98 and a markup of 57.6%. What are the cost and markup dollars?

8. A buyer retails an item for $67.98 and adds markup dollars of $48.97. What is the cost and markup percent?

CHALLENGERS

1. A buyer purchases the following items: a skirt that costs $75.00 and retails for $250.00; a blouse that retails at $38.00 and has a markup percent of 52.6%; a sweater that has markup dollars of $40.00 and a markup percent of 53.8%; a pair of shoes that has a retail of $75.00 and markup dollars of $40.00; a jacket that costs $150.00 and has a markup of 53.8%; and a handbag that costs $45.00 and has markup dollars of $25.00. What are all the price factors involved in these items?

2. A jewelry buyer purchases 3 different styles of bracelets. The first bracelet cost
    $16.00 and she retailed it at $31.00. The second bracelet retailed at $17.00, which
    included her $9.00 markup. The last bracelet retailed at $15.00 and costs $5.00. If she
    purchases ten of each style, what would be the total cost, total retail, and total
    markup dollars for this purchase?

3. A book wholesaler has a group of sale-priced books that are at various costs but sug-
    gests a $9.99 retail for all of the books. What are the markup percent and the markup
    dollars on each group if the costs are as follows:

    Group #1 is $15.00 per dozen
    Group #2 is $16.00 for two dozen
    Group #3 is $17.50 for 3 books
    Group #4 is $12.00 for 4 books

    What would be the markup percent and markup dollars if she retailed them all at
    $12.99?

CHAPTER THREE: SUMMARY

Markup is one of the most crucial concepts in business. The company can generate income only through markup. Understanding is essential to the survival of the business. Only by knowing the inter-relationship of cost, retail reductions, overhead, and profit margin can the company grow. But most importantly, management must remember that mathematics only provides a starting point in establishing the selling price of the merchandise. The final analysis required is whether the customer will pay the price the marketing manager charges for the goods.

KEY TERMS

Complement
Cost
Markup dollars
Markup percent
Retail

CHAPTER FOUR
Markup of Groups

OBJECTIVES

After completing this chapter, you should be able to:

- Understand when pricing principles are used in business.
- Understand that the purchase order is a legally binding contract governing all of the terms of the sale.
- Understand that the purchase order is one form of control used in business.
- Apply the principles learned to a business situation.

CONCEPT

Now that you understand the mechanics and concept of pricing, it is time to use the procedure in the correct setting. You are the buyer for a company. You have gone out into the market to make your purchases for the next season. This usually means that you have gone to a manufacturer's showroom to see the latest styles (line). As you are shown the line, various selling points are discussed:

1. Fabric
2. Color
3. Style
4. Price
5. Advertising
6. Similarities to successful styles last year
7. Delivery dates

While the line is shown, you pick out the items that suit your needs. Factors that you consider are:

1. Business image
2. Target customer wants and needs
3. Visual impact
4. Profitability

When you have selected the items you believe fulfill these needs, you are ready to determine the quantities involved. In deciding the amounts you keep the following in mind:

1. Predicted demand
2. Promotional plans
3. Needs for visual impact
4. Store capacity

Once the quantities are determined, you are ready to write down the selected styles on a purchase order.

This involves the process of grouping the styles together. The most common way of grouping the styles is by **delivery** and **classification**. By keeping all the merchandise from a single manufacturer for one particular delivery date together on one purchase order, it is easier to control.

It is important to know that the purchase order is a legally binding document that covers all of the terms of the sale. Written on the purchase order are:

1. Styles
2. Colors
3. Quantities
4. Sizes
5. Costs
6. Retails
7. Freight terms
8. Advertising agreements
9. Shipping instructions
10. Cash discount terms

If all the terms on the purchase order are agreed upon by both parties, the contract, *once signed*, is legally binding and can be broken only if one of the two parties fails to uphold his or her part of the contract. It is, therefore, extremely important that the purchase order be filled out completely to avoid any misunderstandings. Since maintaining a good relationship between the buyer and the manufacturer is essential to the growth of the business, writing down all of the information legibly and clearly will avoid misunderstandings.

The purchase order usually contains a number of styles listed, each of which has its own markup. Therefore, it is important to total the information at the bottom. By totaling the purchase order and then keeping track only of the totals (instead of each individual style), the business will be controlled more easily. The easier the control process, the more effective it is.

Also, by watching totals, you will have more flexibility. For example, if there is an item that must be carried in your stock but the customer is not willing to pay the mathematical price of the item, you can choose other items in a line that will allow higher markups. This will offset the item that cannot be retailed at a high price.

DEFINITIONS OF TERMS USED IN THIS CHAPTER

Advertising — paid messages in a media by an identified sponsor.

Business Image — the ideals a company stands for and projects to the customer.

Cash Discount — the percentage reduced from the invoice as an incentive for prompt payment.

Extension — the number derived from multiplying the quantity times a unit pricing factor (i.e. cost per unit or retail per unit) also referred to as cost total or retail total.

Freight — the amount of money charged for transporting the goods from the manufacturer to the purchaser.

Grouping of purchases — combining items from one vendor on a single order based on classification and delivery date.

Initial markup — the relationship between total markup dollars and total retail that appears on a single purchase order when the merchandise is first brought into the store expressed as part of 100.

Line — a manufacturer's latest styles for a season.

Market — refers to going out to the various vendors to shop the new lines for a season.

Purchase order — a legally binding document which contains all the terms of the sale between a vendor and a purchaser.

Terms of the Sale — agreements that affect the amount and the timing of the payment to a wholesaler for the purchase.

Visual impact — making a merchandise statement to the customer.

STEPS FOR FINDING INITIAL MARKUP OF GROUPS

1. For each item purchased:

   Multiply quantity × cost per unit = cost extension (cost total)
   Multiply quantity × retail per unit = retail extension (retail total)

2. Add cost extensions to get total cost for purchase.

3. Add retail extensions to get total retail for purchase.

4. total retail − total cost = total markup $

   $$\frac{\text{total markup \$}}{\text{total retail}} = \text{initial markup for purchase \% (key)}$$

****

BASIC MARKUP RULE #3:

When working on a purchase order a decision must be made which markup formula to use. Generally, to save time, use the complement formula when deriving cost or retail.

****

SAMPLE PROBLEM

A buyer purchases the following items and puts them on a single purchase order.

Style	Qty	Description	Unit Cost	Unit Retail	Unit Markup $	Markup %
0001	15	blouses	$15.00			52.6%
0002	20	blouses		$25.00		54.7%
0003	17	blouses			$15.00	53.1%
0004	27	blouses	$17.00	$34.00		

What is the initial markup percent on this purchase order?

STEP 1: Establish all the pricing factors for each of the styles using the markup percent and markup percent complement formulas.

$$\frac{\text{markup \$}}{\text{retail}} = \text{markup \% (key) or } \frac{\text{cost}}{\text{retail}} = \text{markup of complement (key)}$$

STYLE 0001: cost = $15.00   markup % = 52.6

STEP A: Decision:

Cost and markup % only given; use markup % complement formula.

STEP B: Formula to find the markup % complement:

100% − markup % = markup complement

STEP C: Apply numbers to the formula.

100% − 52.6% = 47.4%

STEP D: Markup % complement = 47.4%

PURCHASE ORDER

NO: _____

STORE NAME: _____

DEPT: _____

ORDER DATE: _____

DO NOT SHIP BEFORE: _____

CANCEL IF NOT RECD: _____

VENDOR: _____

ADDRESS: _____

FREIGHT ALLOWANCE: _____

FOB PT: _____

SHIP VIA: _____

TERMS: _____ % EOM

CLASS	DESCRIPTION	STYLE	SIZE	COLOR	TOTAL UNITS	COST EA	COST TOT	RET EA	RET TOT	MU%	MU$
TOTALS											

BUYER'S SIGNATURE: _____

STEP E: Formula:

$$\frac{\text{cost}}{\text{retail}} = \text{markup \% complement (key)}$$

STEP F: Apply numbers to the formula.

$$\frac{\$15.00}{x} = 47\% \text{ (key)}$$

STEP G: Divide to get:

$15.00 \div 47.4$ (% key) = \$31.65

STEP H: Retail = \$31.65 (See p. 62.)

STYLE 0002: retail = \$25.00   markup % = 54.7%

STEP I: Decision:

To save time when finding cost only, use the complement formula.

STEP J: Formula:

100% − markup % = markup % complement

STEP K: Apply numbers to the formula:

100% − 54.7% = 45.3%

STEP L: Formula:

$$\frac{\text{cost}}{\text{retail}} = \text{markup \% complement (key)}$$

STEP M: Apply numbers to the formula.

$$\frac{x}{\$25.00} = 45.3 \text{ (\% key)}$$

STEP N: Multiply to get:

$25.00 \times 45.3\%$ (% key) = \$11.33

STEP O: Cost = \$11.33

STEP P: Place numbers in the correct place on the form.
           (See p. 62.)

STYLE 0003:   markup $ = $15.00   markup % = 53.1%

STEP Q: Basic markup % formula:

$$\frac{markup\ \$}{retail} = markup\ \% \ (key)$$

STEP R: Apply numbers to the formula.

$$\frac{\$15.00}{x} = 53.1\ (\%\ key)$$

STEP S: Divide to get:

$15.00 ÷ 53.1 (% key) = $28.25

STEP T: Retail = $28.25

STEP U: Cost formula:

retail − markup $ = cost

STEP V: Apply numbers to the formula.

$28.25 − $15.00 = $13.25

STEP W: Cost = $13.25

STYLE 0004:   retail = $34.00   cost = $17.00

STEP X: Find markup dollars using the formula.

retail − cost = markup $

STEP Y: Apply numbers to the formula.

$34.00 − $17.00 = $17.00

STEP Z: Markup $ = $17.00

STEP AA: Basic markup % formula:

$$\frac{markup\ \$}{retail} = markup\ \% \ (key)$$

STEP BB: Apply the numbers to the formula.

$$\frac{\$17.00}{\$34.00} = \frac{x}{100}$$

STEP CC: Divide to get:

$$\$17.00 \div \$34.00 \ (\% \ key) = 50.0\%$$

STEP DD: Markup % = 50.0%

Recap of information derived in Step 1 (see p. 62 for information location):

Style	Qty.	Description	Unit Cost	Unit Retail	Unit Markup $	Markup %
0001	15	blouses	$15.00	$ 31.65	$16.65	52.6%
0002	20	blouses	$11.33	$25.00	$13.67	54.7%
0003	17	blouses	$13.25	$28.25	$15.00	53.1%
0004	27	blouses	$17.00	$34.00	$17.00	50.0%

STEP 2:   Find cost extensions.

   STEP EE: Extension formula:

   quantity × cost = cost extension

   STEP FF: Style 0001

   15 × $15.00 = $225.00

   STEP GG: Style 0002

   20 × $11.33 = $226.60

   STEP HH: Style 0003

   17 × $13.25 = $225.25

   STEP II: Style 0004

   27 × $17.00 = $459.00

   STEP JJ: See p. 62, where information has been entered on form.

STEP 3:   Find retail extensions.

   STEP KK: Style 0001

   15 × $31.65 = $474.75

STEP LL: Style 0002

20 x $25.00 = $500.00

*STEP MM:*Style 0003

17 x $28.25 = $480.25

STEP NN: Style 0004

27 × $34.00 = $918.00

STEP 4:   Find the total cost by adding cost extensions together:

$225.00 + $226.60 + $225.25 + $459.00 = $1,135.85

STEP 5:   Find total retail by adding retail extensions together:

$475.75 + $500.00 + $480.25 + $918.00 = $2,374.00

STEP 6:   Figure the markup based on grand totals.

STEP OO: Markup $ formula:

retail – cost = markup $

STEP PP: Apply numbers to the formula.

$2,374.00 – $1,135.85 = $1,238.15

STEP QQ: Markup $ = $1,238.15

STEP RR: Basic markup % formula:

$$\frac{\text{markup \$}}{\text{retail}} = \text{markup \% (key)}$$

STEP SS: Apply numbers to the formula.

$$\frac{\$1,238.15}{\$2,374.00} = \text{x (\% key)}$$

STEP TT: Divide to get:

$1,238.15 ÷ $2,374.00 (% key) = 52.2%

STEP UU: Markup % = 52.2%

(See p. 62 for location of figures on form.)

PURCHASE ORDER

NO: _____

STORE NAME: _____
DEPT: _____
ORDER DATE: _____
DO NOT SHIP BEFORE: _____
CANCEL IF NOT RECD: _____

VENDOR: _____
ADDRESS: _____
FOB PT: _____
SHIP VIA: _____
TERMS: _____ % EOM
FREIGHT ALLOWANCE: _____

CLASS	DESCRIPTION	STYLE	SIZE	COLOR	TOTAL UNITS	COST EA	COST TOT	RET EA	RET TOT	MU%	MU$
	blouses	0001			15	Given $15.00	Step FF $225.00	Step H $31.65	Step KK $474.75	Given 52.6%	Given $16.65
	blouses	0002			20	Step O $11.33	Step GG $226.60	Given $25.00	Step LL $500.00	Given 54.7%	$13.67
	blouses	0003			17	Step W $13.25	Step HH $225.25	Step T $28.25	Step MM $480.25	Given 53.1%	Given $15.00
	blouses	0004			27	Given $17.00	Step II $459.00	Given $34.00	Step NN 918.00	Step DD 50.0%	Step Z $17.00
				TOTALS	79		Step 4 $1,135.85		Step 5 $2,374.00	Step UU 52.2%	Step QQ $1,278.15

BUYER'S SIGNATURE: _____

IN-CLASS PRACTICE PROBLEMS

See purchase orders, pp. 64-67.

PURCHASE ORDER

NO: 6879452

STORE NAME: Ashton's

DEPT: Missy Collection

ORDER DATE: July 19

DO NOT SHIP BEFORE: 9/15

CANCEL IF NOT RECD: 10/12

VENDOR: Pierre C's

ADDRESS: 1914 Sixth Ave.

Burlington, MA

FREIGHT ALLOWANCE: 3%

FOB PT: Store

SHIP VIA: West Coast Trucking

TERMS: 8/10 % EOM

CLASS	DESCRIPTION	STYLE	SIZE	COLOR	TOTAL UNITS	COST EA	COST TOT	RET EA	RET TOT	MU%	MU$
62	Blouses	1234	Assorted		326	$15.00		$35.00			
63	Skirt	1235	Assorted		400	$25.00					$35.00
64	Sweater	1236	Assorted		126	$20.00				61.3%	
65	Coat	1237	Assorted		57			$196.00			$100.00
66	Belt	1238	Assorted		600			$15.00		58.7%	
67	Scarves	1239	Assorted		300					51.3%	$15.00
			TOTALS								

BUYER'S SIGNATURE:

PURCHASE ORDER

NO: 179453

STORE NAME: Kimberley's Klass

DEPT: Books

ORDER DATE: May 12

DO NOT SHIP BEFORE: 6/1

CANCEL IF NOT RECD: 7/5

VENDOR: Golden

ADDRESS: 12345 Park Ave.

New York, NY.

FREIGHT ALLOWANCE: 2%

FOB PT: Factory

SHIP VIA: Common Carrier

TERMS: 2/10 % EOM

CLASS	DESCRIPTION	STYLE	SIZE	COLOR	TOTAL UNITS	COST EA	COST TOT	RET EA	RET TOT	MU%	MU$
31	Dictionary	771			300	$4.50		$9.75			
37	Thesaurus	1869			108	$4.75				46.1%	
29	Flash Cards	373			96	$3.95				51.3%	
TOTALS											

BUYER'S SIGNATURE:

PURCHASE ORDER

NO: 773649

STORE NAME: Warm-up

DEPT: Finger Fantasy

ORDER DATE: January 10

DO NOT SHIP BEFORE: 2/11

CANCEL IF NOT RECD: 2/20

VENDOR: Racers Co.

ADDRESS: 1507 E. Fifth Avenue

New York, NY.

FREIGHT ALLOWANCE: None

FOB PT: Store

SHIP VIA: Western Trucking

TERMS: 2/10 % EOM

CLASS	DESCRIPTION	STYLE	SIZE	COLOR	TOTAL UNITS	COST EA	COST TOT	RET EA	RET TOT	MU%	MU$
78	Mittens	3962	Assorted		57	$48.00-dozen		$8.00			
79	Gloves	4713-4	Assorted		60	$6.75 ea.		$13.00			
			TOTALS								

BUYER'S SIGNATURE:

PURCHASE ORDER

NO: 71596

STORE NAME: Bradley's

DEPT: Budget Dresses

ORDER DATE: 4/1

DO NOT SHIP BEFORE: 4/31

CANCEL IF NOT RECD: 5/15

VENDOR: Jessie's

ADDRESS: 289 Walnut

Los Angeles, CA

FREIGHT ALLOWANCE: None

FOB PT: Store

SHIP VIA: Roadway

TERMS: 8/10 % EOM

CLASS	DESCRIPTION	STYLE	SIZE	COLOR	TOTAL UNITS	COST EA	COST TOT	RET EA	RET TOT	MU%	MU$
72	Dresses	999	Assorted		276	$5.75				52.6%	
84	Dresses	1000	Assorted		562			$17.50		61.4%	
96	Dresses	2000	Assorted		231	$19.50				48.7%	
101	Dresses	3000	Assorted		368			$19.50		50.3%	
	TOTALS										

BUYER'S SIGNATURE:

HOMEWORK

1. Fill in the following chart.

Cost	Retail	Markup $	Markup %
	$ 15.95		47.8%
	$ 17.50		63.75%
	$ 54.85		13.6%
	$1,043.85	$ 546.87	
	$ 34.77	$ 21.75	
$ 2.33			57.8%
$ 4.85			47.8%
$ 7.50			53.8%
$ 39,587.93		$4,837.85	
$ 395.72		$ 75.47	
		$ 76.89	34.8%
		$ 53.98	41.8%

2. A buyer purchases an item at $16.75 cost and plans to take a 38.3% markup. What will his retail and markup dollars be?

3. A buyer purchases 36 television sets costing $259.00 each and takes markup dollars on each television of $358.00. What is her retail and markup percent?

4. The buyer of the men's suit department purchases 18 blazers at $78.50 cost each and retails at $168.00. What are the markup percent and markup dollars?

5. Jane Sorenson, the cosmetics buyer, purchases 34 vanity mirrors that she retails at $68.00, showing a 60.3% markup. What is her cost and markup dollars?

6. The ready-to-wear buyer has 14 dresses left after a sale. Since they were a special purchase (written on a purchase order at a sale price), she notices that her markup dollars on the purchase order were $24.00 per dress and her retail was $8.00 each. Before she adjusts the price, she must figure her cost and markup percent for this style. What were they?

7. On a purchase order for 900 units of an item, a buyer has total markup dollars of $679.00 and an initial markup percent of 63.8%. What were her cost and retail on this order?

Write the following groups on the purchase orders that follow:

8. Group #1

Qty.	Cost	Retail	Markup $	Markup %
14	$23.00	$68.00		
48	$16.99	$46.50		
96	$34.80	$86.50		
465	$23.89	$35.67		

PURCHASE ORDER

NO: _____

STORE NAME: _____

DEPT: _____

ORDER DATE: _____

DO NOT SHIP BEFORE: _____

CANCEL IF NOT RECD: _____

VENDOR: _____

ADDRESS: _____

FREIGHT ALLOWANCE: _____

FOB PT: _____

SHIP VIA: _____

TERMS: _____ % EOM

CLASS	DESCRIPTION	STYLE	SIZE	COLOR	TOTAL UNITS	COST EA	COST TOT	RET EA	RET TOT	MU%	MU$
	TOTALS										

BUYER'S SIGNATURE: _____

9. Group #2

Qty.	Cost	Retail	Markup $	Markup %
68	$4.65	$ 6.58		
36	$6.45	$ 7.69		
17	$3.86	$20.89		
6	$6.93	$17.75		

PURCHASE ORDER

NO: _____

STORE NAME: _____

DEPT: _____

ORDER DATE: _____

DO NOT SHIP BEFORE: _____

CANCEL IF NOT RECD: _____

VENDOR: _____

ADDRESS: _____

FREIGHT ALLOWANCE: _____

FOB PT: _____

SHIP VIA: _____

TERMS: _____ % EOM

CLASS	DESCRIPTION	STYLE	SIZE	COLOR	TOTAL UNITS	COST EA	COST TOT	RET EA	RET TOT	MU%	MU$
TOTALS											

BUYER'S SIGNATURE: _____

10. Group #3

Qty.	Cost	Retail	Markup $	Markup %
177	$ 6.59			40.6%
34	$ 5.78			56.7%
7	$ 3.68			78.9%
67	$18.99			56.9%
19	$23.89			65.9%

PURCHASE ORDER

NO: _____

STORE NAME: _____
DEPT: _____
ORDER DATE: _____
DO NOT SHIP BEFORE: _____
CANCEL IF NOT RECD: _____

VENDOR: _____
ADDRESS: _____

FREIGHT ALLOWANCE: _____
FOB PT: _____
SHIP VIA: _____
TERMS: _____ % EOM

CLASS	DESCRIPTION	STYLE	SIZE	COLOR	TOTAL UNITS	COST EA	COST TOT	RET EA	RET TOT	MU%	MU$
	TOTALS										

BUYER'S SIGNATURE: _____

11. Group #4

Qty.	Cost	Retail	Markup $	Markup %
78		$78.00	$23.00	
26		$80.99	$56.00	
47		$23.56	$15.13	
78		$ 4.58	$ 2.38	
101		$ 7.89	$ 5.67	

PURCHASE ORDER

STORE NAME: _____

DEPT: _____

ORDER DATE: _____

DO NOT SHIP BEFORE: _____

CANCEL IF NOT RECD: _____

VENDOR: _____

ADDRESS: _____

FREIGHT ALLOWANCE: _____

FOB PT: _____

SHIP VIA: _____

TERMS: _____ % EOM

NO: _____

CLASS	DESCRIPTION	STYLE	SIZE	COLOR	TOTAL UNITS	COST EA	COST TOT	RET EA	RET TOT	MU%	MU$
	TOTALS										

BUYER'S SIGNATURE: _____

12. Group #5

Qty.	Cost	Retail	Markup $	Markup %
85		$45.00		54.8%
57		$67.00		60.8%
76		$34.00		67.0%
35		$79.78		63.9%
94		$79.46		98.6%

PURCHASE ORDER

NO: _____

STORE NAME: _____
DEPT: _____
ORDER DATE: _____
DO NOT SHIP BEFORE: _____
CANCEL IF NOT RECD: _____

VENDOR: _____
ADDRESS: _____

FREIGHT ALLOWANCE: _____
FOB PT: _____
SHIP VIA: _____
TERMS: _____ % EOM

CLASS	DESCRIPTION	STYLE	SIZE	COLOR	TOTAL UNITS	COST EA	COST TOT	RET EA	RET TOT	MU%	MU$
TOTALS											

BUYER'S SIGNATURE: _____

13. Group #6

Qty.	Cost	Retail	Markup $	Markup %
457		$14.09		45.8%
23		$59.78		67.9%
74		$69.08		32.9%
49		$15.98		67.9%
23		$59.07		46.1%

PURCHASE ORDER

NO: _____

STORE NAME: _____

DEPT: _____

ORDER DATE: _____

DO NOT SHIP BEFORE: _____

CANCEL IF NOT RECD: _____

VENDOR: _____

ADDRESS: _____

FREIGHT ALLOWANCE: _____

FOB PT: _____

SHIP VIA: _____

TERMS: ____ % EOM

CLASS	DESCRIPTION	STYLE	SIZE	COLOR	TOTAL UNITS	COST EA	COST TOT	RET EA	RET TOT	MU%	MU$
	TOTALS										

BUYER'S SIGNATURE: _____

14. Group #7

Qty.	Cost	Retail	Markup $	Markup %
23	$24.98	$52.98		
89	$23.98		$38.96	
68	$67.90			52.8%
79		$47.98	$21.87	
398		$96.00		45.9%
27			$98.74	87.9%

PURCHASE ORDER

NO: _____

STORE NAME: _____

DEPT: _____

ORDER DATE: _____

DO NOT SHIP BEFORE: _____

CANCEL IF NOT RECD: _____

VENDOR: _____ FREIGHT ALLOWANCE: _____

ADDRESS: _____ FOB PT: _____

SHIP VIA: _____

TERMS: _____ % EOM

CLASS	DESCRIPTION	STYLE	SIZE	COLOR	TOTAL UNITS	COST EA	COST TOT	RET EA	RET TOT	MU%	MU$
TOTALS											

BUYER'S SIGNATURE: _____

CHALLENGER

A buyer reviews her purchases of styles 7261 and 7262 (a basic skirt and blouse) for the spring season. Her purchase were as follows:

1st shipment:

Style	Qty.	Description	Unit Cost	Unit Retail	Unit Markup $	Markup %
7261	500	skirt		$12.75		51.3%
7262	700	blouse		$ 9.25	$10.00	

2nd shipment:

Style	Qty.	Description	Unit Cost	Unit Retail	Unit Markup $	Markup %
7261	250	skirt	$13.00			50.0%
7262	320	blouse	$10.00	$20.00		

3rd shipment:

Style	Qty.	Description	Unit Cost	Unit Retail	Unit Markup $	Markup %
7621	400	skirt		$27.00		50.0%
7262	600	blouse			$12.00	51.3%

What is her markup percent for each purchase order? Given these purchases, what is the markup of style 7261 throughout the spring season? What is the markup of style 7262? (Use following purchase orders.)

PURCHASE ORDER

NO: _____

STORE NAME: _____

DEPT: _____

ORDER DATE: _____

DO NOT SHIP BEFORE: _____

CANCEL IF NOT RECD: _____

VENDOR: _____

ADDRESS: _____

FREIGHT ALLOWANCE: _____

FOB PT: _____

SHIP VIA: _____

TERMS: _____ % EOM

CLASS	DESCRIPTION	STYLE	SIZE	COLOR	TOTAL UNITS	COST EA	COST TOT	RET EA	RET TOT	MU%	MU$
TOTALS											

BUYER'S SIGNATURE: _____

PURCHASE ORDER

STORE NAME: _____   VENDOR: _____   FREIGHT ALLOWANCE: _____   NO: _____

DEPT: _____   ADDRESS: _____   FOB PT: _____

ORDER DATE: _____   SHIP VIA: _____

DO NOT SHIP BEFORE: _____   TERMS: _____ % EOM

CANCEL IF NOT RECD: _____

CLASS	DESCRIPTION	STYLE	SIZE	COLOR	TOTAL UNITS	COST EA	COST TOT	RET EA	RET TOT	MU%	MU$
	TOTALS										

BUYERS SIGNATURE: _____

PURCHASE ORDER

NO: _____

STORE NAME: _____

DEPT: _____

ORDER DATE: _____

DO NOT SHIP BEFORE: _____

CANCEL IF NOT RECD: _____

VENDOR: _____

ADDRESS: _____

FREIGHT ALLOWANCE: _____

FOB PT: _____

SHIP VIA: _____

TERMS: _____ % EOM

CLASS	DESCRIPTION	STYLE	SIZE	COLOR	TOTAL UNITS	COST EA	COST TOT	RET EA	RET TOT	MU%	MU$
TOTALS											

BUYER'S SIGNATURE: _____

CHAPTER FOUR: SUMMARY

Purchase orders are contractual agreements between the manufacturer and the marketing manager. They serve as a guide to ensure that both parties completely understand all the terms of the sale. Through grouping the merchandise on purchase orders by like styles and statements, the retailer creates a blueprint of how the selling floor will look throughout the season. Additionally, from an operational point of view, a clearly written purchase order prevents misunderstandings that damage the relationship between merchant and vendor.

KEY TERMS

Advertising
Business image
Cash discount
Extension
Freight
Grouping of purchases
Initial markup
Line
Market
Purchase order
Terms of the sale
Visual impact

CHAPTER FIVE
Terms of the Sale

OBJECTIVES

After completing this chapter you should be able to:

- Define terms of the sale and the various options available.
- Understand the effect of the terms on profit.
- Identify the business situations that govern terms of the sale.
- Apply the mechanics of terms of the sale to a purchase transaction.

CONCEPT

When a marketing manager purchases merchandise from a wholesaler, many subjects are discussed. Much of the talk is related specifically to the product and the marketing strategy appropriate for the product. Some of the most common topics of discussion are:

1. Benefits derived from the product
2. Options on the product
3. Alterations on the product
4. Special care required by the product
5. Compatibility with target market and store image
6. Delivery dates
7. Cost
8. Suggested retail
9. Exclusivity and break dates
10. Promotional strategies
11. Competitor's strategies

All of these subjects and many more are discussed at this meeting. In the process known as **negotiation**, each person tries to get concessions from the other person in order to benefit the companies represented.

Among the topics discussed are the **terms of the sale**. Terms of the sale are agreements that affect the amount and the timing of the payment to the wholesaler for the purchase. Types of terms are:

1. Trade discount
2. Freight terms
3. Cash discount
4. Dating
5. Quantity discount

Trade discount applies only when wholesalers are allowed to establish the retail price of an item. Working from the suggested list price, a trade discount is offered if the marketing manager agrees to sell the merchandise at the listed price. A trade discount is a percentage or a series of percentages reduced from the list price. By subtracting the percentage from the list price, the invoice (billed) price of the item is established. A series trade discount reduces the cost even further, encouraging reorders. If the wholesaler is prohibited by law from establishing the retail price of an item, he or she will quote wholesale cost. Then the concept of a trade discount does not apply.

The next terms of the sale negotiated are **freight terms.** Because more and more companies today are geographically widening their sources for products, and because transportation prices are rising, the subject of who will pay for the freight charges is of major importance. Basically, the marketing manager wants the wholesaler to pay the freight charges, and the wholesaler wants the reverse. Many companies, in fact, have established freight terms that are not negotiable because of the negative impact of freight charges on profit. However, if the freight terms are negotiable, the wholesaler and retailer must agree on the FOB (free on board) point. The FOB point is the location at which the ownership of the goods changes. From the manufacturer to the FOB point, the manufacturer pays for all of the freight charges. If the shipment is damaged, destroyed, or stolen, the manufacturer assumes the loss and/or contacts the company's insurance carrier to settle with the freight company, if appropriate. From the FOB point to the retailer, the marketing manager pays all of the charges and assumes the loss if the shipment is damaged, destroyed, or stolen, and/or contacts the insurance carrier to settle with the freight company, if appropriate. Any freight charges assumed by the business are considered part of the cost of goods and must be covered in the retail price. Since freight charges become part of the cost of goods, the less freight the business pays, the more profit can be made on the item.

Cash discount is probably the most commonly used component of terms of the sale. Cash discount is the percentage reduced from the invoice (bill for the goods from the wholesaler) as an incentive for prompt payment. Cash discount is usually composed of two parts: the discount terms and the time frame by which the invoice must be paid (e.g., 8/10 ROG/net 30 means the business gets an 8 percent reduction on the total invoice if it is paid within 10 days of the receipt of goods (ROG) and the bill must be paid within 30 days). Since cash discount reduces the cost of the invoice, it increases the profit that can be made on that merchandise.

Dating is an option in the terms of the sale that refers to cash discount. In **dating,** or **advanced dating,** the wholesaler alters the date on the invoice to give the retailer more time to be eligible for the cash discount. An example of advanced dating would be if the merchandise is shipped August 10 with a cash discount of 2/10 EOM/net 60. Under normal circumstances, the invoice would have to be paid within 10 days of the end of the month (EOM), i.e., by September 10 for the business to receive a 2.0% discount off the invoice. Also, the invoice must be paid in full by October 1. However, if an advanced-dating agreement has been worked out and the wholesaler changes the invoice date to September 10 instead of August 10, the business then has one additional month to qualify for the discount and to pay the bill in full. Advanced dating is particularly valuable to companies who want to avoid interest rates on short-term loans to cover low cash flow periods while still allowing the company to maximize profita- ability.

The last option in the terms of the sale is **quantity discount**. This option is simply an incentive offered by the wholesaler to get the market manager to purchase a larger quantity. A percentage, or a series of percentages, are reduced from the cost price based on the amount of merchandise purchased. Quantity discount can be cumulative or non-cumulative, based on the wholesaler's policy. **Cumulative** quantity discounts refer to establishing various purchase levels for the year with greater discounts applied as the year's purchases grow. This form of quantity discount encourages each retailer to purchase a large volume and to return to the same wholesaler to qualify for a larger discount. **Non-cumulative** quantity discounts merely refer to a set discount on a single purchase. This discount is not figured on the year's total purchases.

Many times, several of the options in the terms of the sale are negotiated as a package. The more concessions the retailer gets from the wholesaler, the more profit the retailer makes. However, even though offering concessions costs the wholesaler money, these concessions often allow the wholesaler to sell more merchandise in larger shipments. More large shipments mean lower labor charges in the shipping departments. When you combine lower labor charges with larger sales volume, concessions can actually have a positive effect on the wholesaler's profit.

DEFINITIONS OF TERMS USED IN THIS CHAPTER

Cash discount — the percentage reduced from the invoice as an incentive for prompt payment.

Cumulative quantity discount — a greater percentage reduction given as the business purchases more throughout the year.

Dating — altering the date on the invoice in order to give the business more time to qualify for the cash discount and pay the bill.

EOM — end of month.

FOB (free on board) point — the location at which ownership of the shipment changes.

Freight terms — the amount of transportation charges each party agrees to pay for a purchase.

Invoice — the bill from the wholesaler for the purchase.

Jobber — an individual who purchases large quantities of a single item from a company at a significantly lower price for the purpose of reselling to another company. The jobber usually pays cash.

Negotiating — the conversation between two people which results in an agreement for purchase.

Net invoice charges — the actual amount paid by the business after the terms of the sale are reduced.

Non-cumulative quantity discount — one set percentage that applies only to a single purchase.

Quantity discount — a percent reduction on the cost price for buying more merchandise.

ROG — receipt of goods.

Suggested list price — a listing of merchandise offered by the wholesaler that includes the suggested retail for the items.

Terms of the sale — agreements that affect the amount and the timing of the payment to the wholesaler for the purchase.

Trade discount — a percentage, or a series of percentages, reduced from the suggested list price that establishes the invoice price of the merchandise.

TRADE DISCOUNT FORMULA

$$\frac{\text{trade discount dollars}}{\text{suggested list price}} = \text{trade discount \%}$$

suggested list price − trade discount dollars = net invoice price

SAMPLE PROBLEM

A small leather goods manufacturer offers a trade discount of 45.0% from the suggested list price. What is the cost price for the following items?

Suggested List Price

Style Number	Description	Suggested Retail
1247	clutch	$35.00
2386	billfold	$25.00
9216	checkbook	$45.00

STEP 1:   Trade discount formula:

$$\frac{\text{trade discount dollars}}{\text{suggested list price}} = \text{trade discount \% (key)}$$

STEP 2:   Apply the numbers to the formula.

clutch:

$$\frac{x}{\$35.00} = 45.0\%$$

billfold:

$$\frac{x}{\$25.00} = 45.0\%$$

checkbook:

$$\frac{x}{\$45.00} = 45.0\%$$

STEP 3:   Multiply to get trade discount dollars.

clutch = $15.75

billfold = $11.25

checkbook = $20.25

STEP 4:   Formula for net invoice price:

suggested list price – trade discount dollars = net invoice price

STEP 5:   Apply numbers to the formula.

clutch:

$35.00 – $15.75 = $19.25

billfold:

$25.00 – $11.25 = $13.75

checkbook:

$45.00 – $20.25 = $24.75

IN-CLASS PRACTICE PROBLEMS

1. Fill in the following chart.

Suggested List Price	Trade Discount %	Net Invoice Price
$40.00	25.0%	
$60.00	31.0%	
$75.00		$65.00
$85.00		$32.00
	60.%	$12.00
	47.5%	$16.00

2. A hardware manufacturer offers the following discounts on the suggested list price:

   wholesalers = 60.0% discount
   jobbers   = 53.7% discount
   retailers   = 51.3% discount

   Suggested List Price

   10 D 3" Nails $16.00
   16 D 3 1/2" Nails $17.50

   What is the invoice price for each type of nail to the wholesaler? jobber? retailer?

3. A cosmetics manufacturer offers the following series of discounts:

   first purchase   40.0%
   second purchase 43.0%
   third purchase   45.0%

   If a beauty supply store makes the following purchases from the suggested list price, what would be the net invoice price for each purchase?

   beauty supply store first purchase $28,000.00
   beauty supply store second purchase $18,000.00
   beauty supply store third purchase $32,000.00

4. A fine china wholesaler purchases the following items on the suggested list price, receiving a 60.0% trade discount. What is the invoice price for each item:

starburst place setting	$195.00
golden rim place setting	$225.00
silver rim place setting	$200.00
starburst serving tray	$175.00
starburst salt and pepper set	$ 50.00

FREIGHT TERMS FORMULA

buyer's share + manufacturer's share = freight charges

$$\frac{\text{buyer's share}}{\text{freight charges}} = \text{buyer's freight percentage}$$

$$\frac{\text{manufacturer's share}}{\text{freight charges}} = \text{manufacturer's freight percentage}$$

$$\frac{\text{FOB point}}{\text{distance between manufacturer and business}} = \text{manufacturer's freight percentage}$$

SAMPLE PROBLEM

A manufacturer and a retailer 600 miles apart agree that the freight charges for a shipment will be shared as follows:

Manufacturer pays 60.0%   Retailer pays 40.0%

The total freight charges are $1,575.00. What is the manufacturer's share? retailer's share? FOB point?

STEP 1:   retailer's freight share formula:

$$\frac{\text{retailer's share}}{\text{freight charges}} = \text{retailer's \%}$$

STEP 2:   Apply numbers to the formula.

$$\frac{x}{\$1,575.00} = 40\%$$

STEP 3:   Multiply to get:

$1,575.00 × 40.0% = $630.00

STEP 4:   retailer's share = $630.00

STEP 5:   Freight charges formula:

retailer's share + manufacturer's share = freight charges

STEP 6:   Apply numbers to the formula.

$1,575.00 − $630.00 = $945.00

STEP 7:   manufacturer's share = $945.00

STEP 8:   FOB point formula:

$$\frac{\text{FOB point}}{\text{distance}} = \text{manufacturer's \%}$$

STEP 9:   Apply numbers to the formula.

$$\frac{x}{600} = 60.0\%$$

STEP 10:   Multiply to get:

600 × 60.0% = 360 miles from manufacturer

IN-CLASS PRACTICE PROBLEMS

1. Fill in the following chart.

Retailer's Share $	Retailer's %	Manufacturer's Share $	Manufacturer's %	Freight Charges
$1,675.00		$1,725.00		
$3,294.00		$2,168.00		
	12.0%			$ 4,000.00
	58.0%			$ 5,000.00
			90.0%	$12,000.00
			19.0%	$ 786.00
$ 925.00	16.0%			
$1,076.00	70.0%			
		$ 900.00	50.0%	
		$ 238.00	41.0%	

2. If the FOB point is 800 miles from the manufacturer and 400 miles from the retailer, how have the freight charges been shared in terms of percentages?

3. The freight agreement between a retailer and a manufacturer is as follows:

    Retailer will pay 40.0% of the charges

    Normally, the charges would have been $40.00. However, because the manufacturer ran into production problems he had to send the merchandise by air. As a result, he agreed to pay all freight charges above what the retailer would usually pay. The air shipment charges were $110.00. What did the retailer pay on this shipment? What did the manufacturer pay on this shipment?

CASH DISCOUNT FORMULA

$$\frac{\text{cash discount \$}}{\text{invoice total}} = \text{cash discount \%}$$

invoice total − cash discount $ = net invoice charges

Parts of the cash discount formula:

     a/b c net d
a = percent cash discount
b = number of days
c = time set for cash discount
d = time set when total payment is required

NOTE: Cash discount timing is based on the receiving date of the merchandise in relationship to the 25th of the month. For example, if the merchandise is received any time between June 1 and June 24, the receiving month is June and the cash discount timing deals with the month of June; if the receiving date is June 25-30, the receiving month is July.

SAMPLE PROBLEM

A retailer and a manufacturer agree to cash discount terms of 8/10 EOM net 90. The invoice is $1,576.00. If the goods are received on June 10, what are the net invoice charges? What is the last date to pay the invoice and qualify for the cash discount? What is the last day by which the invoice must be paid?

****

TERMS OF THE SALE RULE #1:

Remember to first determine the receiving month and use the month to establish the cash discount eligibility date and the net payment date.

****

STEP 1:   Parts of cash discount formula:

        a/b c net d

a = percent cash discount
b = number of days
c = time set for cash discount
d = time set when total payment is required

STEP 2:   Apply the numbers to the formula.

8 = percent cash discount
10 = number of days
EOM = time set for cash discount
90 days = time set when total payment is required = 3 months

STEP 3:   Establish receiving month.

Received June 10 = Receiving month June

STEP 4:   Cash discount formula:

$$\frac{\text{cash discount \$}}{\text{invoice total}} = \text{cash discount \%}$$

STEP 5:   Apply numbers to the formula.

$$\frac{x}{\$1,576} = 8.0\%$$

STEP 6:   Multiply to get:

$8.0\% \times \$1,576 = \$126.08$

STEP 7:   Cash discount \$ = \$126.08

STEP 8:   Net invoice charges formula:

Invoice total − cash discounts \$ = net invoice charges

STEP 9:   Apply the numbers to the formula.

$\$1,576 − \$126.08 = \$1,449.92$

STEP 10:   Net invoice charges = $1,449.92

STEP 11:   Determine last day to receive cash discount.

Receiving month is June
Terms are based on EOM of June
Last day to qualify is July 10

STEP 12:   Determine last day to pay invoice in full.

Receiving month is June
90 days for complete payment = 3 months
July = month # 1
August = month #2
September = month # 3

Invoice due: September 30

IN-CLASS PRACTICE PROBLEMS

1. Fill in the following chart.

Total Inv. Charges	Cash Disc. $	Net Inv. Charges	Cash Disc. Terms	Cash Disc. Date	Net Paymt. Date	Recd. Date	Receiving Month
$1,785.00			2/10 EOM net 30			1/16	
$1,946.00			8/10 ROG net 60			3/6	
		$1,057.32	8/10 ROG net 30			1/10	
		$5,378.90	5/10 EOM net 90			1/16	
		$ 657.00	3/10 EOM net 60			2/3	
		$ 578.00	5/10 ROG net 90			5/18	

2. If the cash discount terms on a $6,524.00 invoice received on January 27 are 2/10 EOM net 30, what are the net invoice charges, the last day to be eligible for cash discount, and the last date the invoice must be paid in full?

3. The cash discount terms on lingerie are 3/10 EOM net 60. If a shipment invoiced at $10,586.00 was received on February 7, what are the net invoice charges, the date of eligibility for cash discount, and net payment?

DATING – PROCEDURE

Advanced dating on an invoice establishes **new receiving month**—procedure for date eligibility is same as cash discount based on **new month.**

SAMPLE PROBLEM

A shipment was received on 6/3. Due to an advanced dating agreement, the invoice date was altered to 9/1. If the cash discount terms were 1/10 EOM net 60, what is the new cash discount eligibility date and the date the invoice must be paid based on the advanced dating agreement?

STEP 1:   Advanced dating formula:

Advanced date establishes new receiving month.

STEP 2:   Apply numbers to the formula.

Advanced Date = 9/3—prior to the 25th—receiving month September

STEP 3:   Establish advanced dating cash discount eligibility date.

                 Receiving month is September
                 Terms are based on EOM of September
                 New eligibility date is October 10th.

STEP 4:   Establish last date for total payment with advanced dating.

                 Receiving month is September
                 Net date 60 days = 2 months
                 October = month #1
                 November = month #2

                 Net payment date with advanced dating = November 30

IN-CLASS PRACTICE PROBLEMS

1. Fill in the following chart.

Inv. Charges	Cash Disc. $	Net Inv. Charges	Cash Disc. Terms	Recd. Date	Advance Date	Cash Disc. Elig. Date	Net Date	Rec. Month
$5,000.00			2/10 EOM net 30	1/10	3/10			
		$9,763.00	3/10 EOM net 90	2/3	4/1			
$6,720.00			2/10 EOM net 60	6/9	9/1			

2. A manufacturer alters the invoice date from 5/3 to 7/3, totaling $10,578.00 with a cash discount agreement of 5/10 EOM net 30. What are the net invoice charges and advanced-dating eligibility dates?

3. An invoice shipped on 3/6 has a date of 4/15. How much additional time has the manufacturer given the retailer to qualify for cash discount and net payment?

QUANTITY DISCOUNT FORMULA

$$\frac{\text{quantity discount \$}}{\text{invoice total}} = \text{quantity discount \%}$$

$$\frac{\text{net invoice charges}}{\text{invoice total}} = \text{quantity discount complement}$$

invoice total − quantity discount $ = net invoice charges

SAMPLE PROBLEM

A manufacturer offers a 5.0% discount on a shipment of $5,000.00 or more. A retailer purchases merchandise invoicing for $7,694.00. What are the net invoice charges on this shipment?

STEP 1:   Quantity discount formula:

$$\frac{\text{quantity discount \$}}{\text{invoice total}} = \text{quantity discount \%}$$

STEP 2:   Apply numbers to the formula.

$$\frac{x}{\$7,694.00} = 5.0\%$$

STEP 3:   Multiply to get:

x = $384.70

STEP 4:   Net invoice formula:

invoice total − quantity discount $ = net invoice charges

STEP 5:   Apply the numbers to the formula.

$7,694.00 − $384.70 = $7,309.30

STEP 6:   Net invoice charges = $7,309.30

IN-CLASS PRACTICE PROBLEMS

1. Fill in the following chart.

Invoice Total	Quantity Discount $	Quantity Discount %	Net Invoice
$15,786.30	$ 63.20		
$ 659.32	$ 31.80		
$ 1,546.00		2.3%	
$ 67,394.80		7.9%	
$ 7,138.00			$ 6,254.00
$ 57,932.00			$ 49,876.00
	$136.00	10.0%	
	$285.73	9.0%	
		6.0%	$ 576.00
		3.0%	$ 1,947.00

2. A retailer pays net invoice charges of $789.00 taking a discount of 5.0%. What was the invoice total without discount? What were the discount dollars?

3. A retailer is offered the following series of cumulative quantity discounts:

   Total Purchases of $10,000.00 to $20,000.00 = 10.0% discount
   Total Purchases of $20,001.00 to $35,000.00 = 12.0% discount
   Total Purchases of $35,001.00 to $50,000.00 = 15.0% discount
   Total Purchases of $50,001.00 and greater = 20.0% discount

   He places the following orders:

   Jan 1   Order #1: $10,587.00
   Jan 15   Order #2: $27,000.00
   Jan 30   Order #3: $40,000.00

What are the discount dollars and net charges for each shipment based on the cumulative discount agreement?

CHALLENGER

The terms of the sale for an invoice totaling $10,000.00 shipped on 6/21 with freight charges of $623.00 are as follows:

Retailer Freight Share   =   60.0%
Quantity Discount   =   10.0%
Cash Discount   =   2/10 EOM net 60
Advanced Date   =   8/1

What is the retailer's freight charge? manufacturer's freight charge? quantity discount dollars? net invoice charges after quantity discount? eligibility date for cash discount? eligibility date for net payment? net invoice charges after cash discount and quantity discount? What is the final charge to the retailer, including freight charges?

CHAPTER FIVE: SUMMARY

Negotiating terms of the sale is part of the art of merchandising. Through negotiations the buyer can improve the profit performance of the business while establishing strong relationships with the manufacturer. The manufacturer, on the other hand, can increase the volume of business with each retailer, thereby strengthening the rapport between them. The ideal situation in marketing occurs when both the marketing manager and the manufacturer profit from the transactions.

KEY TERMS

Cash discount
Cumulative quantity discount
Dating
EOM
FOB
Freight terms
Invoice
Jobber
Negotiating
Net invoice charges
Non-cumulative quantity discount
Quantity discount
ROG
Suggested list price
Terms of the sale
Trade discount

CHAPTER SIX
Averaging of Markups

OBJECTIVES

After completing this chapter, you should be able to:

- Understand the concept of offsetting lower markup purchases with higher markup purchases to achieve the markup goal.
- Understand why different merchandise has different markups.
- Understand the terminology involved in averaging of markups.
- Apply the mechanics of averaging of markups to a business situation.

CONCEPT

In Chapter Four, the concept of offsetting purchases having low markups with high markup goods was introduced. This concept, known as **averaging of markups** is essential to achieving the planned markup goal that is crucial to the success of the business. However, before we examine the principles involved in averaging of markups, we must investigate the concept of planning.

To achieve any goal, there must be a plan; to trust in blind luck is generally to resign yourself to failure. By defining your goals and constructing a step-by-step strategy to achieve these goals, you give yourself measurable levels of performance. This is the first step to control. By measuring progress, the marketing manager can take timely action before the goal is lost.

A marketing manager plans to achieve a goal of profit. These plans usually are made for a six-month period, known as the **seasonal plan**. The six-month plan includes *stock levels, sales volume, markdown dollars, planned purchases, markup goals, gross margin goals, and often profit goals*. Because the profit and gross margin goals are contingent upon the markup goals being achieved, it is extremely important for the marketing manager to have some method of ensuring that the markup goal on the plan will be attained.

To do this, merchandise is purchased in such a way that, at the end of the season, the merchandise markup **averages** out to the planned goal. Profit can be assured by controlling the merchandise mix.

However, to control the mix, various factors must be considered that determine the markup of the item. Basically, there are three factors:

1. Different market/different markup
2. Different purpose/different markup
3. Different appeal/different markup

The first factor is called **different market/different markup.** This refers to the situation where *merchandise appeals to different target customers*. This can occur within a store or department or may refer to different types of stores. For example, the marketing manager may choose to buy one particular style of merchandise for the budget customer, taking a lower markup on it to attract the price-conscious customer. On high-fashion merchandise, the marketing manager may take a higher markup because of the risk of obsolescence and because price is not this customer's primary concern. Therefore, by managing the amount of each style purchased, the merchant uses higher-markup fashion goods to offset lower-markup budget goods while still serving the customer's wants and needs.

The second factor is known as **different purpose/different markup**. This refers to the situation where a style of merchandise might be bought at regular price while a month later the same merchandise is bought again for a special event such as a clearance or a sale. In this situation, the first purchase is made earlier in the selling season when the demand for the merchandise is high; therefore, a full markup can be taken. However, on the second purchase of this style, there is a different purpose for the purchase. It is later in the season and the merchandise is bought to be advertised at a lower price to attract traffic to a sale event. Again, just as in the situation of different market/different markup, the merchandise is managed (various quantities are purchased at different markups) to achieve the overall markup goal.

The last factor to consider is **different appeal/different markup**. This situation covers the *appeal of the designer label*. Because of the prestige associated with certain names, the marketing manager can make more money on certain types of merchandise. The fact that the merchandise carries a logo (special label or symbol identifying it) gives the merchandise snob appeal. Most social groups put a value on wearing the "right" thing. The popularity of these items is determined by the socioeconomic group to which it appeals. Therefore, the marketing manager can take advantage of the popularity by pricing the desirable merchandise higher and offsetting some of the lower markups in the stock.

In each of these situations, we have talked about offsetting lower markups with higher markups to achieve the planned goal. Obviously, this method of averaging together is an important one. During each trip to the market, when selecting each style, while writing each purchase order, the marketing manager must keep in mind the overall markup goal and how to achieve it.

The best method of keeping track of markup progress is to form a table with rows for total needed, already bought, and balance-to-buy. **Total needed** represents the planned amount for the situation. This can also be referred to as open-to-buy. **Already bought** is the amount of money already totaled on purchase orders that are signed and processed although not necessarily already shipped and received. **Balance-to-buy** represents the amount remaining to be spent.

This table is similar to a checkbook register in that the balance is brought forward to tell you what you have left to spend. However, unlike the checkbook register, it also tells how the balance must be spent to achieve the goal. The marketing manager can protect the profit by safeguarding the markup goal.

DEFINITIONS OF TERMS USED IN THIS CHAPTER

Already bought — the amount previously purchased that affects the balance-to-buy. Can also be referred to as "already spent" or "already purchased."

Balance-to-buy — the amount remaining to be purchased after the already bought is subtracted from the total needed.

Concepts of averaging — offsetting lower markup purchases with higher markup purchases to achieve the markup goal.

Different appeal/different markup — the process of purchasing and pricing the merchandise that has brand or designer name status.

Different market/different markup — the process of purchasing and pricing the merchandise which appeals to specific social groups.

Different purpose/different markup — the process of purchasing and pricing the merchandise which will be used for regular and store promotional events.

Goals — objectives which are to be achieved.

Open-to-buy — the amount of money the buyer has to spend on new merchandise.

Planning — the process of analyzing the business and establishing the directions and goals of the business.

Purchases — orders placed by the buyer for the business.

Receipts — merchandise that arrives in the store from the manufacturer to fill a purchase order.

Total cost — cost extension.

Total needed — the complete quantity, cost extension, retail extension or markup percent required for a promotion or a given period of time.

Total retail — retail extension.

FORMULAS

total needed − already bought = balance-to-buy

already bought + balance-to-buy = total needed

total needed − balance-to-buy = already bought

$$\frac{\text{markup dollars}}{\text{retail}} = \text{markup percent} \quad OR \quad \frac{\text{cost}}{\text{retail}} = \text{markup percent complement}$$

STEPS TO AVERAGE MARKUPS

STEP 1: Find the markup percent complement for every markup percent given in the problem.

STEP 2: Find the total retail and total cost extensions using markup percent or markup percent complement formula.

STEP 3: Find already-bought cost and retail extensions using the markup percent or markup percent complement formula.

STEP 4:   Subtract extension columns to get balance-to-buy cost and/or retail.

STEP 5:   Find unit cost or retail if requested in the problem.

****

BASIC MARKUP RULE #4

This table (Figure 6-1) does not work at the unit level. If given a unit cost or retail, find the extensions, work the problem, then convert back to the unit level if requested in the problem.

BASIC MARKUP RULE #5

When purchasing for a special event where the unit retail is established for the total need row (i.e., a $9.99 glove sale), then the unit retail is "set" for all rows in the table. The unit retail must be copied down to every row in the table. This rule applies only to unit retail.

****

	Quantity	Unit Cost	Cost Ext.	Unit Retail	Retail Ext.	Markup %	Markup % Complement
Total Needed	Given		Given or Comp. × Retail Ext.		Given or Cost Ext. + Comp.	Given or $\frac{R-C}{R}$	100% − Markup %
Already Bought	Given		Given or Comp. × Ret. Ext.		Given or Cost Ext. Comp.	Given or $\frac{R-C}{R}$	100% − Markup %
Balance to Buy	Tot. Needed − Already Bought	$\frac{Cost\ Ext.}{Qty.}$	Tot. Needed − Already Bought	$\frac{Retail\ Ext.}{Qty.}$	Tot. Needed − Already Bought	$\frac{R-C}{R}$	100% − Markup %

Figure 6-1   comp. = complement

SAMPLE PROBLEMS

---

1.   A buyer's plans for the spring season call for $500,000.00 in retail purchases at a 56.4% markup. She has already bought merchandise amounting to $150,000.00 at cost at a 51.2% markup. What is her balance-to-buy?

STEP 1:   Place all information given in the table (see Figure 6-2).

              A. Total retail needed = $500,000.00

              B. Total markup % needed = 56.4%

C. Already bought cost = $150,000.00

D. Already bought markup % = 51.2%

	Quantity	Unit Cost	Cost Ext.	Unit Retail	Retail Ext.	Markup %	Markup % Complement
Total Needed	0				(A) $500,000.00	(B) 56.4%	
Already Bought			(C) $150,000.00			(D) 51.2%	
Balance-to-Buy							

Figure 6-2

STEP 2: Complete line #1 (total needed) by using the markup percent complement formula to save time (you do not need to know markup dollars).

A. 100% − markup % = markup % complement

B. Apply numbers to the formula.

100% − 56.4% = 43.6%

C. Markup % complement = 43.6%

D. Markup % complement formula:

$\frac{cost}{retail}$ = markup % complement (key)

E. Apply numbers to the formula.

$\frac{x}{\$500,000}$ = 43.6%

F. Multiply to get:

$500,000.00 × 43.6 (% key) = $218,000.00

G. Cost = $218,000.00

H. Place this entry in the correct box on the table (see Figure 6-3).

STEP 3:   Complete line 2 (already bought) by using markup percent formula.

STEP A: Markup % complement:

100% − markup % = complement

STEP B: Apply numbers to the formula.

100% − 51.2% = 48.8%

STEP C: Markup % complement = 48.8%

STEP D: Complement formula:

$$\frac{cost}{retail} = complement\ (\%\ key)$$

STEP E: Apply numbers to the formula.

$$\frac{\$150,000}{x} = 48.8\ (\%\ key)$$

STEP F: Divide to get:

$150,000.00 ÷ 48.8 (% key) = $307,377.05

STEP G: x = $307,377.05

STEP H: Place this entry in the table (see Figure 6-3).

STEP 4:   To find balance-to-buy, use the formula given in this unit.

Total needed − already bought = balance-to-buy

STEP A: Cost

$218,000.00 − $150,000.00 = $68,000.00

STEP B: Retail

$500,000.00 − 307,377.05 = $192,622.95

STEP C: Enter these entries in the correct boxes in the table
(Figure 6-3).

STEP 5:   Figure markup percent for balance-to-buy by using markup percent formula
markup dollars over retail.

STEP A: Retail − cost = markup $

STEP B: Apply numbers to the formula.

$$\$192,622.95 - \$68,000.00 = \$124,622.95$$

STEP C: Markup percent formula:

$$\frac{\text{markup } \$}{\text{retail}} = \text{markup \% (key)}$$

STEP D: Apply numbers to the formula.

$$\frac{\$124,622.95}{\$192,622.95} = x \text{ (\% key)}$$

STEP E: Divide to get:

$$\$124,622.95 \div \$192,622.95 \text{ (\% key)} = 64.7\%$$

STEP F: Markup percent = 64.7%

STEP G: Enter answer on table (see Figure 6-3).

	Quantity	Unit Cost	Cost Ext.	Unit Retail	Retail Ext.	Markup %	Markup % Complement
Total Needed			(STEP 2) $218,000.00		$500,000.00	56.4%	43.6%
Already Bought			$150.000.00		(STEP 3) $307,377.05	51.2%	48.8%
Balance-to-Buy			(STEP 4) $ 68,000.00		(STEP 4) $192,622.95	(STEP 4) 64.7%	35.3%

Figure 6-3

2. **A buyer needs 600 units of accessories for a special $6.99 sale event, but needs a 50.3% markup. She purchases half of the needed units at $3.75 cost each. What is her balance-to-buy and her average cost per unit for the remaining purchase?**

STEP 1:   Place all of the given information on the chart (see Figure 6-4).

NOTE: This problem has a quantity, so you must extend quantity times cost and retail per unit to work it correctly.

NOTE: This problem also sets the retail per unit for the merchandise at $6.99 per unit; therefore, each line in the table will use $6.99 as the unit retail.

A. Place unit retail in the unit retail boxes on each line (total needed, already bought, and balance-to-buy—$6.99).

B. Place total needed markup in the correct box (50.3%).

C. Place total quantity needed in the correct box (600 units).

D. Calculate retail extension for total needed.

quantity × $6.99 = $4,194.00
(use extension to solve problem)

E. Determine already bought units.

600 ÷ 2 = 300

F. Write the unit cost of the merchandise already bought in the corner of the correct box. Unit cost of already bought = $3.75

G. Calculate already bought cost extension.

quantity × unit cost = cost extension

300 x $3.75 = $1,125.00

H. Calculate already bought retail extension.

quantity × unit retail = retail extension

300 × $6.99 = $2,097.00

	Quantity	Unit Cost	Cost Ext.	Unit Retail	Retail Ext.	Markup %	Markup % Complement
Total Needed	600 (STEP C)			$6.99 (STEP A)	$4,194.00 (STEP D)	50.3% (STEP B)	
Already Bought	300 (STEP E)	3.75 (STEP F)	$1,125.00 (STEP G)	$6.99 (STEP A)	$2,097.00 (STEP H)		
Balance-to-Buy				$6.99 (STEP A)			

Figure 6-4

STEP 2:   Complete line 1 (total needed) by using the markup percent complement formula 100% - markup % = markup complement

I. Apply numbers to the formula.

100% − 50.3% = 49.7%

J. Markup percent complement = 49.7%

K. Markup percent complement formula:

$\dfrac{cost}{retail}$ = markup % complement (% key)

L. Apply numbers to the formula.

$\dfrac{x}{\$4,194.00}$ = 49.7 (% key)

M. Multiply to get:

$4,194.00 × 49.7 (% key) = $2,084.42

N. Total needed cost = $2,084.42

Place numbers in the correct box in the table (Figure 6-5).

STEP 3:   Complete row 2 (already bought) by figuring the markup percent using the basic markup percent formula.

Retail − cost = markup $

O. Apply numbers to the formula.

$2,097.00 − $1,125.00 = $972.00

P. Markup dollars = $972.00

Q. Basic markup percent formula:

$\dfrac{markup\ \$}{retail}$ = markup % (key)

R. Apply numbers to the formula.

$\dfrac{\$972.00}{\$2,097.00}$ = x (% key)

S. Divide to get:

$972.00 ÷ $2,097.00 (% key) = 46.4%

T. Already-bought markup percent = 46.4%

(see Figure 6-5)

STEP 4:   Calculate row 3 (balance-to-buy) at cost and retail by subtracting row 2 (already bought) from row 1 (total needed) extensions.

U. Quantity:

   600 (total needed)
  –300 (already bought)
   300 (balance-to-buy)

V. Cost:

$ 2,084.42 (total needed)
 –1,125.00 (already bought)
$ 959.42 (balance-to-buy)

W. Retail:

$ 4,194.00 (total needed)
 –2,097.00 (already bought)
$ 2,097.00 (balance-to-buy)

Place these entries in the table (Figure 6-5).

STEP 5:   Figure the markup percent for line 3 (balance-to-buy) by using the basic markup percent formula.

X. Retail – cost = markup $

Y. Apply numbers to the formula.

$2,097.00 – $959.42 = $1,137.58

Z. Markup dollars = $1,137.58

AA.   Basic markup percent formula:

$$\frac{\text{markup } \$}{\text{retail}}$$

BB.   Apply numbers to the formula.

$$\frac{\$1,137.58}{\$2,097.00} = \frac{x}{100}$$

CC.   Divide to get:

$1,137.58 ÷ $2,097 (% key) = 54.247973%

DD.   Markup % = 54.3%

Place this entry in the correct box in the table (Figure 6-5).

STEP 6:   Figure the average unit cost for the balance-to-buy by dividing quantity into cost extension.

$959.42 ÷ 300 = $3.198

EE.   Average unit cost = $3.20

Place this entry in the correct box (Figure 6-5).

	Quantity	Unit Cost	Cost Ext.	Unit Retail	Retail Ext.	Markup %	Markup % Complement
Total Needed	600 (STEP C)		$2,084.42 (STEP Z)	$6.99 (STEP A)	$4,194.00 (STEP D)	50.3% (STEP B)	
Already Bought	300 (STEP E)	$3.75 (STEP F)	$1,125.00 (STEP G)	$6.99 (STEP A)	$2,097.00 (STEP H)	46.4%	
Balance-to-Buy	300 (STEP A)	$3.20	$ 959.42	$6.99 (STEP A)	$2,097.00	54.3%	

Figure 6-5

IN-CLASS PRACTICE PROBLEMS

1. The notions buyer plans a sale of $150,000.00 retail worth of gifts and novelties at a 54.3% markup. She has already bought 600 units of travel accessories at $6.00 cost and retailed them for $11.99. What is her balance?

2. The toy buyer plans a special promotion of stuffed animals to sell at $7.99. She needs a total of 1,000 units at a 51.8% markup. Her first purchase consisted of 400 units at $4.25 cost per unit. What is her balance-to-buy?

3. The hosiery buyer needs 400 slippers for the anniversary sale, retailing for $12.00 at a 52.0% markup. He has already bought 100 pairs at a cost of $6.50 each. What is his balance-to-buy and the average cost per unit on this balance?

	Quantity	Unit Cost	Cost Ext.	Unit Retail	Retail Ext.	Markup %	Markup % Complement
Total Needed							
Already Bought							
Balance-to-Buy							

	Quantity	Unit Cost	Cost Ext.	Unit Retail	Retail Ext.	Markup %	Markup % Complement
Total Needed							
Already Bought							
Balance-to-Buy							

	Quantity	Unit Cost	Cost Ext.	Unit Retail	Retail Ext.	Markup %	Markup % Complement
Total Needed							
Already Bought							
Balance-to-Buy							

4. The men's clothing buyer has already bought 100 tweed suits at $250.00 each cost and retails them at $550.00 each. With his balance, he is going to purchase 50 herringbone suits at $300.00 cost. His total planned seasonal markup is 54.2%. At what unit retail price must he sell the herringbone suits to achieve his plan?

5. The divisional merchandise manager of the Home Store has a division markup plan of 50.2%. His buyers have already bought $150,000.00 at cost, retailing the merchandise for $285,000.00. The balance is $300,000.00 at retail. What does the cost balance have to be for the buyers to achieve the plan?

6. The coordinates buyer plans a departmental markup of 51.3%. She purchases 100 jackets to retail at $32.00 each with a $16.00 cost. With her balance-to-buy, she now plans to purchase 3,200 skirts at $25.00 retail. What are the numbers, including all unit prices?

	Quantity	Unit Cost	Cost Ext.	Unit Retail	Retail Ext.	Markup %	Markup % Complement
Total Needed							
Already Bought							
Balance-to-Buy							

	Quantity	Unit Cost	Cost Ext.	Unit Retail	Retail Ext.	Markup %	Markup % Complement
Total Needed							
Already Bought							
Balance-to-Buy							

	Quantity	Unit Cost	Cost Ext.	Unit Retail	Retail Ext.	Markup %	Markup % Complement
Total Needed							
Already Bought							
Balance-to-Buy							

7. The buyer for the woolen shop has already bought 180 cashmere pullovers for $50.00 cost each and retails them at $120.00 each. She now wants to spend her balance-to-buy on 150 shetland cardigans that she will retail at $54.00 each. If her total markup plan is 56.8%, how much can she afford to spend on each cardigan?

8. The manager of the Burlington store needs 600 units of shoes that retail at $39.99 each for a sidewalk sale. However, in spite of the sale purchases, the store must maintain a 50.6% markup on total purchases. The buyer has already bought 450 units at a $23.00 cost per unit. What is the maximum cost per unit the buyer can pay for the remaining sale merchandise to allow the manager to achieve the markup goal?

9. The furnishings buyer plans to spend $50,000.00 at retail for the spring sale. However, he must maintain a 51.4% markup on his sale purchases. He purchases 1,000 units of socks at $15.00 per dozen cost to sell at $2.00 each. What is his balance-to-buy?

	Quantity	Unit Cost	Cost Ext.	Unit Retail	Retail Ext.	Markup %	Markup % Complement
Total Needed							
Already Bought							
Balance-to-Buy							

	Quantity	Unit Cost	Cost Ext.	Unit Retail	Retail Ext.	Markup %	Markup % Complement
Total Needed							
Already Bought							
Balance-to-Buy							

	Quantity	Unit Cost	Cost Ext.	Unit Retail	Retail Ext.	Markup %	Markup % Complement
Total Needed							
Already Bought							
Balance-to-Buy							

10. The dress buyer has already bought 600 sundresses at $13.00 cost and retails them for $27.50. She will spend her balance-to-buy on 200 short-sleeved dresses with matching jackets that cost $27.00 each. Her total planned markup is 55.8%. What are the numbers including unit prices?

11. A buyer has total purchases of $115,000.00 at retail for June. His planned markup is 53.0%. His on-order totals $15,000.00 at cost and $32,000.00 at retail. What remains as the balance for the purchases?

12. The cosmetics buyer needs $50,000.00 worth of merchandise at retail for his department for September at a 45.0% markup. He has already written orders totaling $4,875.50 at cost at a 41.3% markup. What is his balance-to-buy?

	Quantity	Unit Cost	Cost Ext.	Unit Retail	Retail Ext.	Markup %	Markup % Complement
Total Needed							
Already Bought							
Balance-to-Buy							

	Quantity	Unit Cost	Cost Ext.	Unit Retail	Retail Ext.	Markup %	Markup % Complement
Total Needed							
Already Bought							
Balance-to-Buy							

	Quantity	Unit Cost	Cost Ext.	Unit Retail	Retail Ext.	Markup %	Markup % Complement
Total Needed							
Already Bought							
Balance-to-Buy							

13. A buyer plans a promotion of 200 jeans to retail at $22.00 each. Her departmental markup plan is 55.2%. Her first purchase consists of 40 units costing $13.00 each. What must be the average unit cost on the balance?

14. The buyer for the junior department must maintain a 56.7% markup on all purchases. She has already bought 150 skirts at $20.00 cost each that she retails at $45.00 each. She is now spending her balance-to-buy on 60 matching sweater vests at $25.00 cost each. What are the numbers including unit prices?

15. The lingerie buyer plans to purchase nightgowns at 54.3% markup totaling $18,500.00 at retail. He buys 300 flannel gowns at $20.00 cost each to retail at $40.00 each. What markup must he now obtain on the balance to achieve his plan?

	Quantity	Unit Cost	Cost Ext.	Unit Retail	Retail Ext.	Markup %	Markup % Complement
Total Needed							
Already Bought							
Balance-to-Buy							

	Quantity	Unit Cost	Cost Ext.	Unit Retail	Retail Ext.	Markup %	Markup % Complement
Total Needed							
Already Bought							
Balance-to-Buy							

	Quantity	Unit Cost	Cost Ext.	Unit Retail	Retail Ext.	Markup %	Markup % Complement
Total Needed							
Already Bought							
Balance-to-Buy							

HOMEWORK

Set up the following in tables and supply all the missing numbers.

1. | Total Quantity | Total Cost | Total Retail |
    |---|---|---|
    | 81 | $981.00 | $1,8968.00 |

Quantity	Already-Purchased Cost	Already-Purchased Retail
24	$9.20 each	$23.00 each

2. | Total Quantity | Total Cost | Total Retail |
    |---|---|---|
    | 68 | $1,400.00 | $2,800.00 |

Quantity	Already-Purchased Cost	Already-Purchased Retail
30	$30.00 each	$50.00 each

3, | Total Quantity | Total Cost | Total Retail |
    |---|---|---|
    | 74 | $1,983.00 | $6,700.00 |

Quantity	Already-purchased cost	Already-purchased retail
48	$20.00 each	$40.00 each

	Quantity	Unit Cost	Cost Ext.	Unit Retail	Retail Ext.	Markup %	Markup % Complement
Total Needed							
Already Bought							
Balance-to-Buy							

	Quantity	Unit Cost	Cost Ext.	Unit Retail	Retail Ext.	Markup %	Markup % Complement
Total Needed							
Already Bought							
Balance-to-Buy							

	Quantity	Unit Cost	Cost Ext.	Unit Retail	Retail Ext.	Markup %	Markup % Complement
Total Needed							
Already Bought							
Balance-to-Buy							

4.

Total Quantity	Total Cost	Total Retail
861	$14,000.00	$77,000.00

Quantity	Already-purchased cost	Already-purchased retail
300	$8.00 each	$25.00 each
200	$10.00 each	$38.00 each

5.

Total Quantity	Total Cost	Total Retail
1,048	$50,000.00	$150,000.00

Quantity	Already-purchased cost	Already-purchased retail
100	$6.36 each	$28.00 each
30	$7.60 each	$25.00 each
40	$8.60 each	$30.00 each
70	$5.00 each	$20.00 each

6.

	Total Cost	Total Retail
	$980.00	$2,000.00
	Already-purchased cost	Already-purchased retail
	$600.00	$1,200.00

	Quantity	Unit Cost	Cost Ext.	Unit Retail	Retail Ext.	Markup %	Markup % Complement
Total Needed							
Already Bought							
Balance-to-Buy							

	Quantity	Unit Cost	Cost Ext.	Unit Retail	Retail Ext.	Markup %	Markup % Complement
Total Needed							
Already Bought							
Balance-to-Buy							

	Quantity	Unit Cost	Cost Ext.	Unit Retail	Retail Ext.	Markup %	Markup % Complement
Total Needed							
Already Bought							
Balance-to-Buy							

7.   Total Cost   Total Retail

     $15.00 $38.00

     Already-purchased cost   Already-purchased retail

     $10.00 $15.00

8.   Total Cost   Total Retail

     $91.00 $300.00

     Already-purchased cost   Already-purchased retail

     $68.00 $100.00

9.   Total Cost   Total Retail

     $750.00 $1,800.00

     Already-purchased cost   Already-purchased retail

     $600.00 $1,200.00

	Quantity	Unit Cost	Cost Ext.	Unit Retail	Retail Ext.	Markup %	Markup % Complement
Total Needed							
Already Bought							
Balance-to-Buy							

	Quantity	Unit Cost	Cost Ext.	Unit Retail	Retail Ext.	Markup %	Markup % Complement
Total Needed							
Already Bought							
Balance-to-Buy							

	Quantity	Unit Cost	Cost Ext.	Unit Retail	Retail Ext.	Markup %	Markup % Complement
Total Needed							
Already Bought							
Balance-to-Buy							

10. A buyer has committed on her yearly stock plans to achieve a markup of 86.0% with planned purchases at cost of $43,000.00. She has already spent $21,000.00 in cost with a markup of 74.0%. She now must show her boss what she will do to achieve her plan.

11. A buyer has $17,000.00 at retail as a balance on her open-to-buy plans and must achieve a 68.0% markup on this balance. Her total plan was $38,000.00 at retail with a 51.0% markup. What is her already-purchased?

12. A buyer has a retail balance of $68,000.00 for a special sale. However, on her total plan she promised her boss to maintain a 62.3% markup for all purchases. She has already purchased $43,000.00 at cost at a 61.8% markup. What was her total plan?

	Quantity	Unit Cost	Cost Ext.	Unit Retail	Retail Ext.	Markup %	Markup % Complement
Total Needed							
Already Bought							
Balance-to-Buy							

	Quantity	Unit Cost	Cost Ext.	Unit Retail	Retail Ext.	Markup %	Markup % Complement
Total Needed							
Already Bought							
Balance-to-Buy							

	Quantity	Unit Cost	Cost Ext.	Unit Retail	Retail Ext.	Markup %	Markup % Complement
Total Needed							
Already Bought							
Balance-to-Buy							

13. A buyer needs 968 units for a new store having a total retail stock plan of $19,400.00 at a 51.6% markup. She has already purchased $7,900.00 cost at a 50.3% markup, leaving her with 157 units yet to purchase. Her best resource offers her a great buy on some closeout goods but she needs to know exactly where she is at this point. Fill in the numbers.

14. A Divisional Merchandise Manager has to show progress on a stretch six-month stock plan to the upper executives who have funded him. His plan was $1,204,000.00 at retail with a 58.0% markup. So far, his buyers have spent $386,000.00 at cost with a 56.8% markup. Fill in the numbers for his presentation.

	Quantity	Unit Cost	Cost Ext.	Unit Retail	Retail Ext.	Markup %	Markup % Complement
Total Needed							
Already Bought							
Balance-to-Buy							

	Quantity	Unit Cost	Cost Ext.	Unit Retail	Retail Ext.	Markup %	Markup % Complement
Total Needed							
Already Bought							
Balance-to-Buy							

CHALLENGERS

1. A buyer's spring plan is $63,000.00 at retail with a 53.8% markup. She spends $12,000.00 at retail achieving her planned markup on her Paris buying trip. When she returns from the trip, her boss informs her that her Spring plan has been revised to a 55.0% markup with a $48,300.00 cost. With the purchases she has already made, what must she now do to achieve her plan?

2. A sales plan of $78,000.00 cost is given with a $300,000.00 retail. Halfway through the season, the buyer is called in because she has spent 75.0% of her retail dollars and is missing her markup plan on these purchases by 1.3%. What must she do on her remaining purchases?

3. A divisional merchandise manager is looking over his buyers' plans and sees that one of his buyers has only $16,000.00 in cost remaining of a $345,000.00 retail total. The buyer's total planned markup is 54.0% but he has only attained a 53.2% markup on purchases to date. In a note to the buyer, what would the DMM write as the numbers involved?

	Quantity	Unit Cost	Cost Ext.	Unit Retail	Retail Ext.	Markup %	Markup % Complement
Total Needed							
Already Bought							
Balance-to-Buy							

	Quantity	Unit Cost	Cost Ext.	Unit Retail	Retail Ext.	Markup %	Markup % Complement
Total Needed							
Already Bought							
Balance-to-Buy							

	Quantity	Unit Cost	Cost Ext.	Unit Retail	Retail Ext.	Markup %	Markup % Complement
Total Needed							
Already Bought							
Balance-to-Buy							

4. A manager is reviewing the stock and sales plan that he received from his buyer. He sees his planned retail stock level is $64,000.00 at a planned markup of 54.0%. But looking at his current on-order, he sees that he has only $20,000.00 at cost with a markup of 51.0%. Before he calls the buyer, he wants to have all his numbers ready to avoid communication problems.

5. A General Merchandise Manager is checking a Divisional Merchandise Manager's performance report and sees that her men's divisional has spent 85.0% of his retail open-to-buy for the year and is missing his markup plan by 5.2%. Since the GMM has given special funding to this DMM to increase the business, approving the planned purchases of $234,000.00 retail with a promise to achieve a 60.0% markup, she calls the DMM in to discuss the problem. What is the nature of the problem? (Supply all numbers).

6. Total planned cost = $34,800.00; total planned retail = $98,600.00; already-bought cost = $10,000.00; already-bought markup = 51.8%.

	Quantity	Unit Cost	Cost Ext.	Unit Retail	Retail Ext.	Markup %	Markup % Complement
Total Needed							
Already Bought							
Balance-to-Buy							

	Quantity	Unit Cost	Cost Ext.	Unit Retail	Retail Ext.	Markup %	Markup % Complement
Total Needed							
Already Bought							
Balance-to-Buy							

	Quantity	Unit Cost	Cost Ext.	Unit Retail	Retail Ext.	Markup %	Markup % Complement
Total Needed							
Already Bought							
Balance-to-Buy							

7.   A buyer needs 376 units to retail at $8.99 each. She must maintain a 50.3% markup
     for this purchase. She buys half of the units at $6.00 cost each. What is the average
     cost of the remaining purchase?

8.   One hundred suits are offered to a buyer at $65.00 cost each. Half of the suits
     should be retailed at $150.00 each, and an additional quarter of the suits should be
     retailed at $140.00 each. To maintain an overall 60.0% markup, what should the
     remaining suits retail?

9.   A buyer has a maintained markup agreement with Jonathan Loman for the spring
     season of 56.8% based on a $150,000.00 cost purchase. She is going to finish her
     purchases having to date spent 66.0% of her retail purchases at 55.0% markup.
     What must she do to achieve this agreement?

	Quantity	Unit Cost	Cost Ext.	Unit Retail	Retail Ext.	Markup %	Markup % Complement
Total Needed							
Already Bought							
Balance-to-Buy							

	Quantity	Unit Cost	Cost Ext.	Unit Retail	Retail Ext.	Markup %	Markup % Complement
Total Needed							
Already Bought							
Balance-to-Buy							

	Quantity	Unit Cost	Cost Ext.	Unit Retail	Retail Ext.	Markup %	Markup % Complement
Total Needed							
Already Bought							
Balance-to-Buy							

10. **Total cost = $25,000.00, markup = 65.9%, balance-to-buy retail = $40,000.00, markup = 70.1%**

	Quantity	Unit Cost	Cost Ext.	Unit Retail	Retail Ext.	Markup %	Markup % Complement
Total Needed							
Already Bought							
Balance-to-Buy							

CHAPTER SIX: SUMMARY

Because different merchandise purchased will have different markups, it is essential to have a means of offsetting the lower markups with higher markups. The method of averaging markups allows the marketing manager to be constantly aware of his or her position, regarding the markup goal. Corrective action (varying the merchandise mix) can be taken in time if the markup performance is constantly monitored. Achieving the planned markup allows the business to be profitable and survive.

KEY TERMS

Already bought
Balance-to-buy
Concept of averaging
Different appeal/different markup
Different market/different markup
Different purpose/different markup
Goals
Open-to-buy
Planning
Purchases
Receipts
Total cost
Total needed
Total retail

CHAPTER SEVEN
Midterm Review

PURPOSE

This chapter provides a review of the merchandising mathematics concepts studied to date.

1. Formulas

PERCENTAGE

$$\frac{part}{whole} = part \ \% \ (key)$$

PERCENT INCREASE/DECRASE

new amoun t + *or* − $ difference = original amount

original amount + *or* − $ difference = new amount

new amount − original amount = $ difference

$$\frac{\$ \ difference}{original \ amount} = \% \ increase/decrease \ (key) \quad OR \quad \frac{new \ amount}{original \ amount} = \begin{array}{c} 100\% + inc \\ or \\ 100\% - dec \end{array}$$

MARKUP

cost + markup $ = retail

retail − markup $ = cost

retail − cost = markup $

$$\frac{markup \ \$}{retail} = markup \ \% \ (key)$$

$$\frac{cost}{retail} = markup \ \% \ complement \ (key)$$

_____

NOTE: This formula is *never* used when both cost and retail are known.

TO FIND MARKUP PERCENT OF GROUP

1. For each item:

    Multiply quantity × cost per unit = cost extension (total cost)

    Multiply quantity × retail per unit = retail extension (total retail)

2. Add cost extension to get total cost for purchase.

3. Add retail extension to get total retail for purchase.

4. (Total retail − total cost)

    $$\frac{\text{total markup dollars}}{\text{total retail}} = \text{markup percent}$$

STEPS FOR AVERAGING MARKUPS

1. Find markup percent complement for every markup percent given in the problem.

2. Find total retail and/or total cost using markup percent or markup percent complement formulas.

3. Find already-bought retail and/or cost using the markup percent or markup percent complement formula.

4. Subtract extension columns to get balance-to-buy cost and/or retail.

5. Find unit cost or retail if requested in problem.

DEFINITIONS

Review all definitions given to date.

IN-CLASS PRACTICE PROBLEMS
(See end of this chapter to check your answers.)

1. Find the total markup percent for the following purchases in the jewelry department. (Use purchase order on p. 156.)

15 dozen bracelets -	cost $36.00 per dozen -	retail $7.50 each
12 dozen necklaces -	cost $66.00 per dozen -	retail $12.50 each
14 dozen earrings -	cost $3.75 each -	retail $8.00 each
16 dozen rings -	cost $25.00 each -	retail $45.00 each

2. A buyer purchases skirts at $180.00 per dozen. What would the retail price be if her markup goal is 54.8%?

3. A buyer wants to purchase dresses to retail at $17.75 each; her markup is 51.0%. What is the maximum cost she can pay to make her markup plan?

4. The suggested retail price on a pair of shorts is $17.50 each. The cost is $102.00 per dozen. What is the markup percent on these shorts?

5. The men's trousers buyer purchases 300 tweeds at $65.00 cost each and 200 plaids at $74.00 cost each. His planned overall markup is 52.3%. If the buyer retails the tweeds at $130.00, what would be the minimum retail on the plaids if he is to achieve his plan? (Use averaging form on p. 157.)

6. A buyer plans to buy 600 travel kits from Korea for the annual 2-for-$15.00 promotion. His planned markup for this event is 53.2%. If he pays $3.75 cost for the first 300 units, what is the maximum cost per unit on the remainder? (Use averaging form on p. 157.)

7. A buyer purchases a close-out of scarves (280 units) for $2,100.00 total cost. If she prices 60 of the scarves at $25.00 each, 45 units at $22.50, and the remainder at $30.00 each, what markup percent will she have on this purchase? (Use averaging form on p. 157.)

8. A buyer plans to purchase 850 suits to retail at $49.99 each for the spring sale. She needs a 51.3% markup on the total purchase. From one vendor, she buys 400 suits that cost $28.00. Show his buying plan including the unit cost for the balance. (Use averaging form on p. 158.)

9. On an Asian buying trip, a dress shirt buyer plans to spend $60,000.00 cost at a 62.6% markup. In Hong Kong, he places orders of $8,600.00 at cost. He plans to retail these orders at a 60.4% markup. What must he achieve on his balance? (Use averaging form on p. 158.)

10. An outerwear buyer plans a 51.2% markup on his purchases. He buys 30 ski jackets at $150.00 cost and retails them for $325.00. He now plans to spend his balance on 50 leather coats at $175.00 cost. What should be the retail on the leather coats to achieve his plan? (Use averaging form on p. 158.)

11. A young-junior sportswear buyer buys 600 sweaters for a special promotion to be marked up 52.0%. She plans to mark them all at the same retail price. If she pays $12.50 for 350 of them, and $10.00 for the remainder, what should the retail price be? (Use averaging form on page 159.)

12. The blouse buyer plans to buy $60,000.00 at retail for the month of January. She needs a 54.3% markup. On January 10th, she totals up her orders and finds she has $15,000.00 cost and $40,000.00 retail. What is her balance? (Use averaging form on p. 159.)

13. A buyer purchases toddler close-outs consisting of 300 rompers at $40.00 a dozen and 500 T-shirts at $3.25 each. She wants to retail all this merchandise at the same price. If she needs a 51.9% markup on this purchase, what must the unit retail be? (Use averaging form on p. 159.)

14. A computer buyer whose departmental markup is 50.7% was offered a close-out on software as follows: 200 units of General Ledger at $300.00 each cost, and 500 units of Time Calendar Management at $325.00 each cost. If he retails both of these items at the same price and achieves his markup percent on the total order, what would his unit retail be? (Use averaging form on p. 160.)

15. The pillow buyer needs $120,000.00 retail worth of down pillows for next fall. His department plan markup is 51.0%. He places orders of $42,000.00 cost with a retail of $86,000.00. What is his balance? (Use averaging form on p. 160.)

16. The women's shoe buyer buys the new Manhattan line of sandal. She buys 65 of style #6201 at $25.00 cost with a $62.00 retail. She now is considering buying 130 of style #7108, which costs $31.50. If she must achieve a 56.2% markup on all purchases, what is the minimum retail for style 7108? (Us averaging form on p. 160.)

17. An assistant is purchasing for her coat classification. She plans to spend $30,000.00 at retail from this vendor. She buys 200 coats at $50.00 cost and marks them up 51.8%. If her classification plan includes a planned markup of 52.0%, what is her balance? (Use averaging form on p.161.)

18. The candy buyer needs 400 one-pound boxes of Valentine candy for the month of February. The boxes are to retail for $17.50 each. She purchases 150 boxes at $12.00 each. If her planned markup is 49.7%, what is her balance? (Use averaging form on p. 161.)

19. The men's shoe buyer purchases the following items:

     200 loafers at $36.00 cost, to retail at $80.00
     400 slip-ons at $4.00 cost, getting a 52.3% markup
     350 lace-ups at $120.00 retail, getting a 56.2% markup

     What is the markup percent on the total? (Use the purchase order on p. 162.)

20. The junior sportswear buyer purchases 65 jumpsuits, getting a 58.7% markup with $37.00 each markup dollars. What are the unit cost and unit retail?

21. What would be the cost of an item that retails at $12.00 based on the following departmental markups?

piece goods	49.8%
accessories	52.7%
ties	59.8%
furniture	41.3%
cosmetics	43.7%

22. The shirt buyer purchases 180 white short-sleeved shirts at $108.00 a dozen and retails them at a 51.6% markup. He then buys 200 pastel long-sleeved shirts with $15.00 in markup dollars and a 52.3% markup. Last, he purchases 280 plaids at $36.00 retail with a 55.0% markup. What is the markup percent of the group? (Use purchase order on p. 163.)

PURCHASE ORDER

STORE NAME: _____

DEPT: _____

ORDER DATE: _____

DO NOT SHIP BEFORE: _____

CANCEL IF NOT RECD: _____

VENDOR: _____

ADDRESS: _____

FREIGHT ALLOWANCE: _____

FOB PT: _____

SHIP VIA: _____

TERMS: _____ % EOM

NO: _____

CLASS	DESCRIPTION	STYLE	SIZE	COLOR	TOTAL UNITS	COST EA	COST TOT	RET EA	RET TOT	MU%	MU$
	TOTALS										

BUYER'S SIGNATURE: _____

	Quantity	Unit Cost	Cost Ext.	Unit Retail	Retail Ext.	Markup %
Total Needed						
Already Bought						
Balance-to-Buy						

	Quantity	Unit Cost	Cost Ext.	Unit Retail	Retail Ext.	Markup %
Total Needed						
Already Bought						
Balance-to-Buy						

	Quantity	Unit Cost	Cost Ext.	Unit Retail	Retail Ext.	Markup %
Total Needed						
Already Bought						
Balance-to-Buy						

	Quantity	Unit Cost	Cost Ext.	Unit Retail	Retail Ext.	Markup %
Total Needed						
Already Bought						
Balance-to-Buy						

	Quantity	Unit Cost	Cost Ext.	Unit Retail	Retail Ext.	Markup %
Total Needed						
Already Bought						
Balance-to-Buy						

	Quantity	Unit Cost	Cost Ext.	Unit Retail	Retail Ext.	Markup %
Total Needed						
Already Bought						
Balance-to-Buy						

	Quantity	Unit Cost	Cost Ext.	Unit Retail	Retail Ext.	Markup %
Total Needed						
Already Bought						
Balance-to-Buy						

	Quantity	Unit Cost	Cost Ext.	Unit Retail	Retail Ext.	Markup %
Total Needed						
Already Bought						
Balance-to-Buy						

	Quantity	Unit Cost	Cost Ext.	Unit Retail	Retail Ext.	Markup %
Total Needed						
Already Bought						
Balance-to-Buy						

	Quantity	Unit Cost	Cost Ext.	Unit Retail	Retail Ext.	Markup %
Total Needed						
Already Bought						
Balance-to-Buy						

	Quantity	Unit Cost	Cost Ext.	Unit Retail	Retail Ext.	Markup %
Total Needed						
Already Bought						
Balance-to-Buy						

	Quantity	Unit Cost	Cost Ext.	Unit Retail	Retail Ext.	Markup %
Total Needed						
Already Bought						
Balance-to-Buy						

	Quantity	Unit Cost	Cost Ext.	Unit Retail	Retail Ext.	Markup %
Total Needed						
Already Bought						
Balance-to-Buy						

	Quantity	Unit Cost	Cost Ext.	Unit Retail	Retail Ext.	Markup %
Total Needed						
Already Bought						
Balance-to-Buy						

PURCHASE ORDER

NO: _____

STORE NAME: _____

DEPT: _____

ORDER DATE: _____

DO NOT SHIP BEFORE: _____

CANCEL IF NOT RECD: _____

VENDOR: _____

ADDRESS: _____

FREIGHT ALLOWANCE: _____

FOB PT: _____

SHIP VIA: _____

TERMS: _____ % EOM

CLASS	DESCRIPTION	STYLE	SIZE	COLOR	TOTAL UNITS	COST EA	COST TOT	RET EA	RET TOT	MU%	MU$
TOTALS											

BUYER'S SIGNATURE: _____

PURCHASE ORDER

NO: _____

STORE NAME: _____

DEPT: _____   VENDOR: _____   FREIGHT ALLOWANCE: _____

ORDER DATE: _____   ADDRESS: _____   FOB PT: _____

DO NOT SHIP BEFORE: _____   SHIP VIA: _____

CANCEL IF NOT RECD: _____   TERMS: _____ % EOM

CLASS	DESCRIPTION	STYLE	SIZE	COLOR	TOTAL UNITS	COST EA	COST TOT	RET EA	RET TOT	MU%	MU$
	TOTALS										

BUYER'S SIGNATURE: _____

MIDTERM REVIEW ANSWER SHEET

PURPOSE

To provide the student with answers to the midterm and final review problems.

MIDTERM REVIEW ANSWERS

1. See purchase order on p. 168.

2. $\dfrac{C}{R}$ = comp % key

   100% − 54.8% = 45.2%

   180.00 ÷ 12 = $15.00 cost per unit

   $\dfrac{15}{x}$ = 45.2%

   Retail = $33.19

3. Shortcut

   $\dfrac{C}{R}$ = comp % key

   $\dfrac{x}{\$17.75}$ = 49.0%

   100% − 51.0% = 49.0% comp

   Cost = $8.70

4. $\dfrac{\text{markup \$}}{R}$ = markup %

   $\dfrac{9}{\$17.50}$ = x%

   $102.00 ÷ 12 = $ 8.50 cost per unit

   $17.50 − $8.50 = $9.00
   R   −   C = markup $

   Markup = 51.4%

5. See averaging form on p. 169.

6. See averaging form on p. 169.

7. $\dfrac{\text{markup \$}}{\text{R}}$ = markup %

   cost tot. = $2,100.00

   $60 \times 25 = 12,500.00$
   $45 \times 22.50 = 1,102.50$
   $175 \times 30 = \underline{5250.00}$
   $\$7,762.50$ total retail

   $7,762.50 - 2,100.00 = \$5,662.50$
   $\text{R}\text{C}\text{markup \$}$

   $\dfrac{5,662.50}{7,762.50} = \text{x}\%$

   Markup % = 73.0%

8. See averaging form on p. 169.

9. See averaging form on p. 170.

10. See averaging form on p. 170.

11. $\dfrac{\text{C}}{\text{R}}$ = comp %

    $14,322.92 \div 600 = \$23.87$

    $350 \times 12.50 = 4,375.00$
    $250 \times 10.00 = \underline{2,500.00}$
    $\$6,875.00$ total cost

    $100\% - 52.0\% = 48.0\%$ comp

    $\dfrac{6875}{\text{x}} = 48.0\%$

    total retail = $14,322.92

    unit retail = $23.87

12. See averaging form on p. 170.

13. See averaging form on p. 171.

    $\dfrac{\text{C}}{\text{R}}$ = comp %

14. $200 \times 300 = \quad 60{,}000$
    $\underline{500 \times 325 = \quad 162{,}500}$
    $\overline{700} \qquad \quad \$222{,}500$
    total units total cost

$451{,}318.45 \div 700 = \$644.74$

$100 - 50.7 = 49.3$

$\dfrac{222{,}500}{x} = 49.3\% = \$45{,}138.45$

unit retail = \$644.74

15. See averaging form on p. 171.

16. See averaging form on p. 171.

17. See averaging form on p. 172.

18. See averaging form on p. 172.

19. See purchase order on p. 173.

20. $\dfrac{\text{markup } \$}{R} = \text{markup } \%$

$\dfrac{\$37.00}{x} = 58.7\% = \$63.03$

$\$63.03 - \$37.00 = \$26.03$
$\quad R \ - \text{markup } \$ \ = C$

Cost = \$26.03
Retail = \$63.03

21. $\dfrac{C}{R} = \text{comp } \%$

Piece Goods

$100\% - 49.8\% = 50.2\% = \text{comp}$

$\dfrac{x}{12} = 50.2\% = \$6.024$

otc4c to

Accessories

$100\% - 52.7\% = 47.3\%$

$\dfrac{x}{12} = 47.3\% = \$5.676$

Ties

$100\% - 59.8\% = 40.2\%$

$\dfrac{x}{12} = 40.2\% = \$4.824$

Furniture

$100\% - 41.3\% = 58.7\%$

$\dfrac{x}{12} = 58.7\% = \$7.044$

Cosmetics

$100\% - 43.7\% = 56.3\%$

$\dfrac{x}{12} = 56.3\% = \$6.756$

Piece Goods	=	$6.02
Accessories	=	$5.68
Ties	=	$4.82
Furniture	=	$7.04
Cosmetics	=	$6.76

22. See purchase order on p.174.

PURCHASE ORDER

STORE NAME: _____   VENDOR: _____   FREIGHT ALLOWANCE: _____   NO: _____

DEPT: _____   ADDRESS: _____   FOB PT: _____

ORDER DATE: _____   SHIP VIA: _____

DO NOT SHIP BEFORE: _____   TERMS: _____ % EOM

CANCEL IF NOT RECD: _____

CLASS	DESCRIPTION	STYLE	SIZE	COLOR	TOTAL UNITS	COST EA	COST TOT	RET EA	RET TOT	MU%	MU$
	bracelets				180	$3.00	$540.00	$7.50	$1,350.00	60.0%	
	necklaces				144	$5.50	$792.00	$12.50	$1,800.00	56.0%	
	earrings				168	$3.75	$630.00	$8.00	$1,344.00	53.1%	
	rings				192	$25.00	$4800.00	$45.00	$8,640.00	44.5%	
	TOTALS				684		$6,762.00		$13,134.00		48.5%

BUYER'S SIGNATURE: _____

	Quantity	Cost	Retail	Markup %
Total Needed	500	$34,300.00	$71,907.76	(comp 47.7%) 52.3%
Already Purchased	300	(65.00 ea) $19,500.00	(130.00 ea) $39,000.00	50.0%
Balance-to-Buy	200	($74.00 ea) $14,800.00	($164.54 ea) $32,907.76	55.0%

	Quantity	Cost	Retail	Markup %
Total Needed	600	$2,106.00	($7.50 ea) $4,500.00	(comp 46.8%) 53.7%
Already Purchased	300	($3.75 ea) $1,125.00	($7.50 ea) $2,250.00	50.0%
Balance-to-Buy	300	($3.27 ea) $981.00	($7.50 ea) $2,250.00	56.4%

	Quantity	Cost	Retail	Markup %
Total Needed	850	$20,693.36	($49.99 ea) $42,491.50	(comp 48.7) 51.3%
Already Purchased	400	($28.00 ea) $11,200.00	($49.99 ea) $19,996.00	44.0%
Balance-to-Buy	450	($21.10 ea) $9,493.36	($49.99 ea) $22,495.50	57.8%

	Quantity	Cost	Retail	Markup %
Total Needed		$60,000.00	$160,427.80	(comp 37.4%) 62.6%
Already Purchased		$8,600.00	$21,717.17	(comp 39.6%) 60.4%
Balance-to-Buy		$51,400.00	$138,710.63	63.0%

	Quantity	Cost	Retail	Markup %
Total Needed	80	$13,250.00	$27,151.64	(comp 48.8%) 51.2%
Already Purchased	30	($150.00 ea) $4,500.00	($325.00 ea) $9,750.00	53.9%
Balance-to-Buy	50	($175.00 ea) $8,750.00	($348.03 ea) $17,401.64	49.7%

	Quantity	Cost	Retail	Markup %
Total Needed		$27,420.00	$60,000.00	(comp 45.7%) 54.3%
Already Purchased		$15,000.00	$40,000.00	62.5%
Balance-to-Buy		$12,420.00	$20,000.00	37.9%

	Quantity	Cost	Retail	Markup %
Total Needed	800	$2,625.00	($6.82 ea) $5,457.38	(comp 48.1%) 51.9%
Already Purchased	300	($40.00 doz) $1,000.00	($6.82 ea) $2,046.00	51.1%
Balance-to-Buy	500	$1,625.00	($6.82 ea) $3,411.38	52.4%

	Quantity	Cost	Retail	Markup %
Total Needed		$58,800.00	$120,000.00	(comp 49.0%) 51.0%
Already Purchased		$42,000.00	$86,000.00	51.2%
Balance-to-Buy		$16,800.00	$34,000.00	50.6%

	Quantity	Cost	Retail	Markup %
Total Needed	195	$5,720.00	$13,059.36	(comp 43.8%) 56.2%
Already Purchased	65	($25.00 ea) $1,625.00	($62.00 ea) $4,030.00	59.7%
Balance-to-Buy	130	($31.50 ea) $4,095.00	($64.46) $9,029.36	54.7%

	Quantity	Cost	Retail	Markup %
Total Needed		$14,400.00	$30,000.00	(comp 48.0%) 52.0%
Already Purchased	200	($50.00 ea) $10,000.00	$20,746.89	(comp 48.2%) 51.8%
Balance-to-Buy		$4,400.00	$9,253.11	52.5%

	Quantity	Cost	Retail	Markup %
Total Nereded	400	$3,521.00	($17.50 ea) $7,000.00	(comp 50.3%) 49.7%
Already Purchased	150	($12.00 ea) $1,800.00	($17.50 ea) $2,625.00	31.4%
Balance-to-Buy	250	($6.88 ea) $1,721.00	($17.50 ea) $4,375.00	60.7%

FIDM PURCHASE ORDER

STORE NAME: _____

DEPT: _____

ORDER DATE: _____

DO NOT SHIP BEFORE: _____

CANCEL IF NOT RECD: _____

VENDOR: _____

ADDRESS: _____

TERMS: _____ % _____ EOM _____ NET _____ EXTRA _____ OTHER

FREIGHT ALLOWANCE: _____

FOB PT: _____ SHIP PT: _____

SHIP VIA: _____

NO: _____

CLASS	DESCRIPTION	STYLE	SIZE	COLOR	TOTAL UNITS	COST EA	COST TOT	RET EA	RET TOT	MU%	COMP
	loafers				200	$36.00	$7,200.00	$80.00	$16,000.00	55.0%	
	slip-ons				400	$40.00	$16,000.00	$83.86	$33,544.00	52.3%	(47.7%)
	lace-ups				350	$52.56	$18,396.00	$120.00	$42,000.00	56.2%	(43.8%)
	TOTALS				950		$41,596.00		$91,544.00	54.6%	

BUYER'S SIGNATURE: _____

FIDM PURCHASE ORDER

STORE NAME: _____

DEPT: _____

ORDER DATE: _____

DO NOT SHIP BEFORE: _____

CANCEL IF NOT RECD: _____

VENDOR: _____

ADDRESS: _____

TERMS: _____ % _____ EOM _____ NET _____ EXTRA _____ OTHER

FREIGHT ALLOWANCE: _____

FOB PT: _____ SHIP PT: _____

SHIP VIA: _____

NO: _____

CLASS	DESCRIPTION	STYLE	SIZE	COLOR	TOTAL UNITS	COST EA	COST TOT	RET EA	RET TOT	MU%	MU$	COMP
	white short-sleeved				180	$9.00	$1,620.00	$18.60	$3,348.00	51.6%		48.4%
	pastel long-sleeved				200	$13.68	$2,736.00	$28.68	$5,736.00	52.3%	$15.00	
					280	$16.20	$4,536.00	$36.00	$10,080.00	55.0%		45.0%
	TOTALS				660		$8,892.00		$19,164.00	53.6%		

BUYER'S SIGNATURE: _____

PART THREE: REPRICING AND INVENTORY

CHAPTER EIGHT
Repricing of Merchandise —
Markdown and Employee Discount

OBJECTIVES

After completing this chapter, you should be able to:

- Understand the concept, causes, and reasons for repricing.
- Understand the difference between markdowns, employee discount, additional markup, markdown cancellation, and markup cancellation.
- Understand the effect each type of repricing has on profit.
- Apply the mechanics of repricing to a business situation.

CONCEPT

As we discussed in Chapter Six, planning is essential to the success of any business. Before markdowns are discussed, more detailed discussion is required about the elements and procedures of the planning process in merchandise marketing.

The first subject to discuss is the **four-five-four fiscal calendar.** This calendar divides the year into four thirteen-week quarters. In each quarter, the first month will have four weeks, the second month will have five weeks assigned to it, regardless of the actual calendar date (e.g., March 1st and 2nd could be "in" the month of February); and the third month will have four weeks. This pattern is carried through each quarter.

The significance of the four-five-four calendar can be seen in regard to planning if we look at the pattern of events in each month of a quarter. For example: the months of the first quarter are February, March, and April. This is called the **spring quarter**. The merchandise received in February and March will be from the manufacturer's spring line. However, May starts the **summer quarter.** Therefore, to clear the stock of spring merchandise, most retailers have a major clearance or sale in April. Once the merchandise has been cleared, the marketing manager has sufficient open-to-buy (money to spend on new merchandise) to bring in the summer line. This merchandise would be received in May and June. Then in July, to prepare for the fall season, the store would have another major clearance to clean out the summer line of merchandise. This cycle repeats for the **fall quarter** (August, September, and October), and the **holiday quarter** (November, December, January).

This pattern of receiving goods and clearing them to make way for new goods introduces the subject of repricing. Repricing involves changing the retail price of an item. The most common form of repricing is markdown.

The concept of markdown involves lowering the retail price of goods to a more salable level. Lowering the retail price decreases the markup dollars and, therefore, has an adverse effect on profit. Since markdown reduces profit, it is extremely important to understand the causes and reasons for markdowns.

There are seven basic causes of markdowns. Markdowns occur because the marketing manager:

1. Accepts goods after cancellation date.
2. Buys goods that do not meet the wants and needs of the target market.
3. Has obsolete fashion goods in stock.
4. Buys wrong-quality merchandise.
5. Receives seasonal merchandise late.
6. Buys into a declining product cycle.
7. Fails to consider customer acceptance when pricing.

All of the above causes can be summed up into one word—*overbuying*.

The *reasons* for taking markdowns are simple:

1. To get rid of seasonal or unsalable merchandise.
2. To clear out remaining odds and ends.
3. To meet a competitor's price on a piece-by-piece basis.

Remember that markdowns are really the marketing manager's last resort to getting rid of merchandise. Display techniques, promotion, exchange, and vendor returns must all be investigated as alternatives before the markdown is taken. If, however, markdown is the only option left, it is essential to take it quickly and reduce the price enough to make the merchandise sell on the first markdown.

Because it is necessary to keep track of inventory levels to avoid out-of-stock situations and excess taxes, marketing managers must keep a record of **all** markdown transactions. To do this, the marketing manager fills out a **price change form.** This form lists the original retail price, the markdown dollars (the amount of dollars reduced from the original retail), the markdown price (the new, lower selling price), and the markdown dollar extension (quantity times the markdown dollars per unit).

Like the markup, which is controlled, markdowns are planned and controlled. Since markdowns hurt profits, it is important to have a plan and not exceed the planned markdown dollars. Therefore, it is common procedure to compare the actual performance (the amount of markdown dollars taken from the price change forms) to the planned markdown.

Another common form of repricing is employee discount. Again, this is a reduction of the retail, but this reduction is given only to employees as a benefit for working for the company.

There are two reasons stores offer employee discount. The first is so that the employee can serve as free advertising for the merchandise carried by the company. In the case of soft goods (apparel and accessories), the company uses the employee as a model by having him or her wear the merchandise so that the customer can see how it looks on a real person. The second reason is as an inexpensive from of training in product knowledge. Through personal use of the merchandise, the employee will know more about the item and have a more informative sales approach.

Like markdowns, employee discount has an adverse effect on profit. However, it has a positive effect on employee morale and sales. It is, in effect, a "Catch 22" in that it has both positive and negative effects.

To maintain records of these discounts, sales to employees are rung into the register by a special code and often have to be approved by a supervisor to protect against possible fraudulent discount use by customers who are not employees.

Other less common types of repricing are **additional markup (AMU), markup cancellations (MUC), and markdown cancellations (MDC).** These price changes apply to special situations.

Additional markup is used when an item is being purchased for a store at a particular cost price and is then reordered. However, during the time between the initial order and the reorder, the cost price of the item has been raised. In order to maintain the markup percentage of the business, the marketing manager raises the retail. When the merchandise arrives in the store, the new merchandise will be retailed differently from the old merchandise. If this situation is not corrected, customers could be upset by the fact that the store does not have the merchandise in his or her particular size at the lower price.

To avoid having to explain a cost price increase, the marketing manager instructs the business manager to take an additional markup on the old merchandise, thereby having the same selling price on all of that item in stock. The additional markup raises the selling price on the goods and can have a positive effect on profit in that there was a lower cost price but a larger retail.

A **markup cancellation** is controlled by law to prevent the marketing manager from fraudulently misrepresenting the value of the merchandise. A markup cancellation occurs when the marketing manager is offered a reorder of merchandise already carried in the store, but at a lower cost price as an incentive to buy a large amount. If the marketing manager decides to take advantage of this purchase, he or she can choose to bring the merchandise in at the sale price or can opt for a markup cancellation. If the latter option is chosen, the merchandise will be received into the store at the original order selling price, therefore getting an inflated markup. Then at sale time (the merchandise must be on the selling floor at least 30 days but no more than 90 days), the marketing manager can cancel the inflated markup, reducing the price. Because the merchandise is purchased at a special incentive price at cost, a markup cancellation provides the retailer a tremendous opportunity to improve profit if the merchandise is sold at the higher retail. However, if the majority of the merchandise is sold at the lower retail price, there is essentially no negative effect on the profit because the markup percent at the sale price is equal to the prevailing department markup percent.

The last type of repricing is the **markdown cancellation**. This is used when merchandise that is always carried in the store (basic stock) is offered for a periodic sale (e.g., pajama sales, underwear sales, hosiery sales). Sale merchandise is brought in to supplement the existing stock in this merchandise. The existing stock is marked down to the sale price to make sure all the merchandise is priced the same. After the sale is over, the marketing manager then cancels the markdown (raises the price back to the original retail). Since a markdown cancellation increases the retail of the item, it has a positive effect on profit.

As you can see, understanding price changes is an integral part of being a marketing manager. It is critical that all price changes are recorded so that an accurate assessment of the stock level can be made at all times.

DEFINITIONS OF TERMS USED IN THIS CHAPTER

Actual — the real dollar amount that occurs in a department to be compared to the plan; the real income.

Additional markup — an upward adjustment of the retail price of old stock due to a cost increase on the recorder.

Causes of markdowns — why markdowns occur such as poor quality, poor operational control, or misjudgment.

Clearance sale — a promotional event where the majority of the merchandise offered is markdown merchandise and not special purchase.

Difference — also known as markdown dollars.

Discount dollars — the amount of money reduced from the original retail price to create the discount price.

Discount price — the adjusted amount of money charged to the employee for the goods.

Employee discount — an employee benefit that entitles the purchaser to buy merchandise at a reduced retail price.

Employee discount percent — the relationship between employee discount dollars and original retail expressed as part of 100.

Fall quarter — August, September, October.

Four-five-four calendar — a fiscal calendar that divides the year into four 13 week quarters.

Holiday quarter — November, December and January. Also known as Winter quarter.

Markdown — the repricing of an item to obtain a lower retail that is salable.

Markdown cancellation — returning regular merchandise to the original retail after a special sale.

Markdown dollars — the amount of money reduced from the original retail to obtain the new retail known as the markdown price.

Markdown price — the reduced price that is derived after making an adjustment of the original retail and that is offered to the customer, also known as "new retail".

Markup cancellation — purchasing merchandise at sale price from the manufacturer and retailing it for short period at an inflated markup with the intention of marking it down at sale time.

Overbuying — buying more merchandise than required by customer demand.

Plan — the dollar goals a buyer establishes to ensure a profitable department; the income strategy of a company.

Price change form — form used to record transactions which adjust the retail price of an item.

Reasons for markdowns — why the marketing manager takes markdowns such as clearance, competition, or promotional purposes.

Retail — the price the buyer charges the ultimate consumer for the merchandise.

Retail sales — the dollar amount of customer purchases.

Special purchase — when the merchandise is bought at sale price from the manufacturer.

Spring quarter — February, March, and April.

Summer quarter — May, June, and July.

FORMULA

Markdown Formulas:

markdown price + markdown \$ = retail

retail − markdown price = markdown \$

retail = markdown \$ = markdown price

$\dfrac{\text{markup \$}}{\text{retail}}$ = markup % (key)	$\dfrac{\text{markdown \$}}{\text{retail sales}}$ = markdown % (key)
$\dfrac{\text{cost}}{\text{retail}}$ = markup % complement (key)	$\dfrac{\text{markdown price}}{\text{retail sales}}$ = markdown % complement (key)

****

BASIC MARKDOWN RULE #1:

When only given markdown price and markdown percent, use the markdown percent complement formula to solve the problem.

BASIC MARKDOWN RULE #2:

To save time when working on a price change form, use the complement formula to find the markdown price when the retail and markdown percent are known.

****

****

BASIC MARKDOWN RULE #3:

When figuring markdown dollars for a department or store, use basic formula but insert the word **sales** after retail (e.g., markdown dollars over **retail sales** = markdown % (key))

****

SAMPLE PROBLEMS

A. A buyer has a poor-selling style currently retailing at $15.00. She plans to reduce this item to a new markdown price of $12.0909. What is the amount of her markdown dollars and her markdown percent?

STEP 1: Formula:

retail − markdown price = markdown $

STEP 2: Apply numbers to the formula.

$15.00 − 12.99 = $2.01

STEP 3: Markdown $ = $2.01

STEP 4: Formula:

$$\frac{\text{markdown \$}}{\text{retail (sales)}} = \text{markdown \% (key)}$$

STEP 5: Apply numbers to the formula.

$$\frac{2.01}{15.00} = x \,(\% \text{ key})$$

STEP 6: Divide to get:

2.01 ÷ 15.00 (% key) = 13.4

STEP 7: Markdown % = 13.4%

B. **A buyer's sales for the month of December are $60,000 with planned markdowns of 8.0%. She actually takes $10,000.00 in December. What is the percent and dollar difference between actual and plan?**

NOTE: The best way to deal with this problem is to split it into three parts: plan, actual, and the comparison of the plan to actual.

PLAN	ACTUAL
STEP 1: Formula: $$\frac{\text{markdown \$}}{\text{retail}} = \text{markdown \% (key)}$$ STEP 2: Apply numbers. $$\frac{x}{60,000} = 8\% \text{ (key)}$$ STEP 3: Multiply: $$60,000 \times 8 \text{ (\% key)}$$ STEP 4: Plan markdown % = $4,800.00	STEP 1: Formula: $$\frac{\text{markdown \$}}{\text{retail}} = \text{markdown \% (key)}$$ STEP 2: Apply numbers. $$\frac{10,000}{60,000} = x \text{ (key)}$$ STEP 3: Divide to get 16.7%. STEP 4: Actual markdown % = 16.7%

COMPARISON
STEP 1: Subtract actual markdown $ from planned markdown $. $4,800 − $10,000 = $5,200.00 STEP 2: Actually took $5,200.00 more in markdown $. STEP 3: Subtract actual markdown % from planned markdown %. 8.0% − 16.7% = −8.7% STEP 4: Actually took 8.7% more markdowns than planned.

IN-CLASS PRACTICE PROBLEMS

1. In the fall season, the furniture buyer took markdown dollars of $50,000.00 on a sales total of $850,000.00. What is the markdown percent?

2. A dress manufacturer found a style in her stock that was not selling at the original price of $48.00. She decided to take a 33.3% markdown to clear her stock of the problem. What are the markdown dollars per unit and the markdown price?

3. The seasonal markdown plan for Department 500 is 13.8%. This percentage was based on sales of $205,000.00. At the end of the season, the divisional merchandise manager looks at her markdown register and discovers that the buyer for this department actually took $33,000.00 in markdowns. Prepare the numbers for her note to the buyer discussing the comparison of plan versus actual. Is this note to be congratulatory in nature or a reprimand for performance?

4. Metcalfe's Grocery Store's March sales totaled $100,000.00. The markdowns were $1,200.00. What is the markdown percent?

5. A coat that originally retailed at $105.00 was marked down to $45.00. What are the new markdown dollars? the markdown percent?

FORMULA FOR EMPLOYEE DISCOUNT

Discount Formulas:

original retail − discount price = discount $

original retail − discount $ = discount price

discount $ + discount price = original retail

$$\frac{\text{discount \$}}{\text{retail (sales)}} = \text{discount \% (key)}$$

$$\frac{\text{discount price}}{\text{retail (sales)}} = \text{discount \% complement (key)}$$

****

BASIC DISCOUNT RULE #1:

When given only discount price and discount percent, use the discount percent complement to solve the problem.

BASIC DISCOUNT RULE #2:

Use the complement formula to find the discount price when the retail and discount percent are known.

BASIC DISCOUNT RULE #3:

When figuring discount dollars for a department or a store, use the same formula but insert the word *sales* after retail (e.g., discount dollars over retail sales = discount percent).

****

SAMPLE PROBLEM

An employee is entitled to a 25.0% discount on an item retailing for $150.00. What are the discount dollars and the discount price for this item?

STEP 1:   Formula:

$$\frac{\text{discount \$}}{\text{retail}} = \text{discount \% (key)}$$

STEP 2:   Apply numbers to the formula.

$$\frac{x}{\$150.00} = 25.0\% \text{ (key)}$$

STEP 3:   Multiply to get:

150×25 (% key) = $37.50

STEP 4:   Discount $ = $37.50

STEP 5:   Formula:

retail − discount $ = discount price

STEP 6:   Apply numbers to the formula.

$150.00 − $37.50 = $112.50

STEP 7:   Discount price = $112.50

IN-CLASS PRACTICE PROBLEMS

1.   An employee is entitled to a 10% discount on his purchases. He buys a can opener for $39.95, a pair of shoes for $109.00, and a shirt for $33.00. What are the discount dollars for each item, the discount price for each item, and the total amount of the sale after discount and before sales tax?

2. A large pharmacy chain's six-month plan shows employee discounts of $6,000.00 on sales of $150,000.00. If the buyer makes her sales plan and actually has discounts of $4,500.00, what is the difference between the actual discount percent and the planned discount percent?

3. A set of golf clubs that retails for $225.00 is sold to an employee who gets $22.50 off in discount dollars. What is the discount percent?

4. The appliance department showed a 14.5% discount of $45,000.00 for the month of June. What are the department retail sales?

MARKDOWN OF GROUPS — EQUATION

STEP 1:   For each item involved, extend markdown dollars (multiply quantity × markdown dollars per item).

STEP 2:   Total all the markdown dollars per style downward to grand total markdown dollars.

STEP 3:   If total markdown percent is required, extend all retails to get total retails per style.

STEP 4:   Add all retail extensions downward to get grand total.

STEP 5: $\dfrac{\text{total markdowns}}{\text{total retail}}$ = markdown % (key)

PRICE CHANGE

NO.: _____
DATE: _____
STORE: _____
DEPT.: _____

Indicate type of price change with an X.
Use separate sheet for each type of change.

X _____ Markdown
_____ Markdown Cancellation
_____ Markup
_____ Markup Cancellation

CLASS	MFG	DESCRIPTION	UNITS	OLD RET	NEW RET	DIFFERENCE Old Retail– New Retail	EXTENSION Quantity × Difference	MD% MD$/Old Retail
Given								
						TOTAL		

SIGNATURE: _____

SAMPLE PROBLEM

A. A buyer has the following merchandise to mark down:

Style #	Qty	Retail	Markdown price	Markdown $	Markdown %
6235	38	$16.00			33.3%
7134	40			$15.00	25.3%
1600	15		$14.99		40.0%
4233	7	$33.00	$21.00		

What were the total markdown dollars and percent of the group?

STEP 1: Place all given numbers in the form (See Figure 8-1 on p. 191).

STEP 2: Provide all the missing numbers by style using the markdown percent formulas.

$$\frac{\text{markdown \$}}{\text{retail}} = \text{markdown \% (key)}$$

or

$$\frac{\text{markdown price}}{\text{retail}} = \text{markdown \% complement (key)}$$

Style 6235

Given:

retail = $16.00

markdown % = 33.3%

STEP A: $\dfrac{x}{\$16.00} = 33.3\%$ (key)

STEP B: Multiply to get:

x = $5.33

STEP C: markdown $ = $5.33 (see Figure 8-1.)

STEP D: Retail − markdown \$ = markdown price

$16.00 − \$5.33 = \$10.67 (See p. 191.)

Style 7134

Given:

markdown dollars = \$15.00

markdown percent = 25.3%

STEP E: $\dfrac{\$15.00}{x} = 25.3\%$ (key)

STEP F: Divide to get:

$x = \$59.29$

STEP G: Retail = \$59.29 (See p. 191.)

STEP H: Retail − markdown \$ = markdown price

STEP I: \$59.29 − \$15.00 = \$44.29 (See p. 191.)

Style 1600

Given:

markdown price = \$14.99

markdown percent = 40.0%

STEP J: Use complement.

100% − 40% = 60.0%

STEP K: Set up formula.

$\dfrac{\$14.99}{x} = 60.0\%$ (key)

STEP L: Divide to get:

$x = \$24.98$

STEP M: Retail = \$24.98

STEP N: Retail – markdown price = markdown $

$24.98 – $14.99 = $9.99 (See p. 191.)

Style 4233

Given:

retail = $33.00

markdown price = $21.00

STEP O: Retail – markdown price = markdown $

$33.00 – $21.00 = $12.00 (See p. 191.)

STEP 3:   Extend all the markdown $ for each style by multiplying quantity x markdown $.

Style 6235   38 × $ 5.33 = $ 202.54 (See p. 191.)

Style 7134   40 × $15.00 = $ 600.00 (See p. 191.)

Style 1600   15 × $ 9.99 = $ 149.85 (See p. 191.)

Style 4233   7 × $12.00 = $ 84.00 (See p. 191.)

STEP 4:   Add extensions to get grand total markdown $.

$202.54 + $600.00 + $149.85 + $84.00 = $1,036.39

STEP 5:   Extend retail by style by multiplying quantity × retail per unit.

Style 6234:   38 × $16.00 = $ 608.00

Style 7134:   40 × $59.29 = $2,371.60

Style 1600:   15 × $24.98 = $ 374.70

Style 4233:   7 × $33.00 = $ 231.00

STEP 6:   Total all retail extensions.

$608.00 + $2,371.60 + 374.70 + $321.00 = $3,585.30

STEP 7:   Using markdown percent formula, figure total markdown percent.

$$\frac{\$1,036.39}{\$3,585.30} = x \ (\% \ key)$$

STEP 8:   Divide to get: x = 28.9%

STEP 9:   Markdown percent = 28.9% (See p. 191.)

PRICE CHANGE

NO : _____
DATE: _____
STORE: _____
DEPT: _____

Indicate type of price change with an X.
Use separate sheet for each type of change.

X   Markdown
_____ Markdown Cancellation
_____ Markup
_____ Markup Cancellation

CLASS	MFG	DESCRIPTION	UNITS	OLD RET	NEW RET	DIFFERENCE	EXTENSION	MD%
		#6235	38	Step 1 $16.00	Step 2 $10.67 step D	Step 2 $5.33 step C	Step 3 $202.54	
		#7134	40	Step 2 $59.29 step I	Step 2 $44.29 step I	Step 1 $15.00	Step 3 $600.00	
		#1600	15	Step 2 $24.98 step M	Step 1 $14.99	Step 2 $9.99 step N	Step 3 $149.85	
		#4233	7	step 1 $33.00	step 1 $21.00	step 2 $12.00 step O	step 3 $84.00	
						TOTAL	$1,036.39 step 4	28.9% step 9

SIGNATURE: _____

IN-CLASS PRACTICE PROBLEMS

Fill in price change forms on pp. 193-196. Figure markdown dollars and markdown percent for each group.

PRICE CHANGE

NO: 4269
DATE: 6/4
STORE: Barkley
DEPT: 280

Indicate type of price change with an X.
Use separate sheet for each type of change.

X	Markdown
	Markdown Cancellation
	Markup
	Markup Cancellation

CLASS	MFG	DESCRIPTION	UNITS	OLD RET	NEW RET	DIFFERENCE	EXTENSION	MD%
36	0043	Scarf	636	$16.00				25.3%
38	0043	Scarf	15		$38.99	$9.01		
42	5217	Barette	491		$17.99			15.3%
61	8691	Sunglasses	360			$7.01		12.3%
98	6363	Hat	91	$21.00		$4.01		
						TOTAL		

SIGNATURE: _____

PRICE CHANGE

NO.: 4268

DATE: 6/4

STORE: Greenwood

DEPT: 9/124

Indicate type of price change with an X.
Use separate sheet for each type of change.

X   Markdown

_____ Markdown Cancellation

_____ Markup

_____ Markup Cancellation

CLASS	MFG	DESCRIPTION	UNITS	OLD RET	NEW RET	DIFFERENCE	EXTENSION	MD%
19	5268	Electric Fan	65	$56.00	$36.99			
22	5314	Hairdryer	136	$35.00	$21.99			
31	5912	Curling Iron	12	$45.00	$32.99			
					TOTAL		

SIGNATURE: _____

PRICE CHANGE

NO.: 0038

DATE: 7/6

STORE: Bentley

DEPT: 040

Indicate type of price change with an X.
Use separate sheet for each type of change.

X	Markdown
	Markdown Cancellation
	Markup
	Markup Cancellation

CLASS	MFG	DESCRIPTION	UNITS	OLD RET	NEW RET	DIFFERENCE	EXTENSION	MD%
90	0462	televisions	3	$1,000.00				25.3%
58	0928	"	16	$1,600.00				31.8%
41	4000	"	2		$1,999.00			15.8%
17	1600	"	9		$999.99			41.8%
						TOTAL		

SIGNATURE: _____

PRICE CHANGE

NO: ___04621___

DATE: ___9.3___

STORE: ___Underwood___

DEPT: ___155___

Indicate type of price change with an X.
Use separate sheet for each type of change.

X	Markdown
	Markdown Cancellation
	Markup
	Markup Cancellation

CLASS	MFG	DESCRIPTION	UNITS	OLD RET	NEW RET	DIFFERENCE	EXTENSION	MD%
55	0060	Bracelet	36			$12.01		29.8%
56	0060	Necklace	21			$16.01		31.3%
57	0060	Rings	12			$7.01		41.8%
58	0060	Pins	6			$9.21		38.6%
					TOTAL			

SIGNATURE: _____

HOMEWORK

1. Markdowns. Fill in the numbers required.

Retail	Markdown Price	Markdown $	Markdown %
$14.00		$5.00	
$25.00		$16.00	
$9.99			33.0%
$7.49			15.0%
$56.80	$25.60		
$9.43	$3.10		
$8.62			51.0%
$121.50		$50.60	
$73.80	$42.80		
$89.80			60.0%
		$7.50	20.0%
		$8.50	35.0%
	$18.40	$12.60	

2. A buyer's sales are $500,000.00 and she plans a 12.1% markdown. She has taken $100,000.00 in markdown dollars to date. Is she going to make her plan? What is the percent and dollar difference between plan and actual?

3. A buyer plans to take 8.0% markdowns in the spring on planned sales of $152,000.00. She also plans for the fall season to take $50,000.00 worth of markdown on $432,000.00 in sales. What is her dollar amount of markdowns in spring? her markdown percent in fall? her total markdown dollars and percent for the entire year?

4. A buyer has $96,200.00 in retail sales with an 8.0% markdown rate. What is the dollar markdown for his department?

5. For the same buyer listed in problem 4 above, the employee discount is 3.0%. What is the dollar employee discount?

6. What are the total dollars for 4 and 5 above? What is the total percent?

7. Fill in the following chart.

Retail	Discount Price	Discount %	Discount %
$15.00	$14.00		
$38.00	$16.00		
$130.00			15.3%
$91.00			17.2%
	$17.50		31.8%
	$19.93		54.6%
$48.00		$4.50	
$17.00		$5.65	
	$14.78	$4.32	
	$16.88	$6.38	
		$16.83	22.8%

8. An employee purchases merchandise utilizing his 35.0% discount. For the first item, he paid $67.80 discount price; for the second item, he paid a discount price of $51.63; and for the third item, he paid a discount price of $23.50. What were the original retails of these three items?

9. A buyer has sales of $65,000.00 for the first quarter. During this time, he had employee discounts of 7.6%. For the second quarter, he had sales of $100,000.00 with employee discounts totaling $12,000.00. What was the dollar amount of discounts for the first quarter? the percent discount for the second quarter? the dollar and percent for the first half of the year?

10. A buyer has the following items to be marked down. Use the form provided to fill in the blanks.

Style	Qty.	Retail	Markdown price	Markdown $	Markdown %
0001	56	$15.00			12.0%
0002	134		$ 3.00		30.0%
0003	12			$16.00	50.0%
0004	17	$16.00	$10.99		
0005	23	$25.00		$12.50	
0006	15		$ 7.99	$ 4.01	

PRICE CHANGE

Indicate type of price change with an X.
Use separate sheet for each type of change.

X _____ Markdown
_____ Markdown Cancellation
_____ Markup
_____ Markup Cancellation

NO.: _____
DATE: _____
STORE: _____
DEPT.: _____

CLASS	MFG	DESCRIPTION	UNITS	OLD RET	NEW RET	DIFFERENCE	EXTENSION	MD%
						Old Retail– New Retail	Quantity x Difference	MD$ / Old Retail
Given			↑					
						TOTAL		

SIGNATURE: _____

CHALLENGER

A buyer takes $125.00 off a cashmere coat in markdown dollars, making the new retail $1,000.00. She has 72 units of this style coat and is allowed $7,500.00 in markdowns in this classification. If she only takes this item in markdowns within the class, will she make her plan? What are the dollars and percent difference between what she is supposed to take and what the markdown on the coats will total?

CHAPTER EIGHT: SUMMARY

Repricing is an integral part of marketing. The causes and reasons for repricing are numerous and are based on business practices, flow of stock based on the four-five-four calendar, and marketing decisions. The important point is to know how repricing affects the business in terms of profit and to establish control methods that provide a means for taking corrective action on a timely basis.

KEY TERMS

Actual
Additional markup
Causes of markdowns
Clearance sale
Difference
Discount dollars
Discount price
Employee discount
Employee discount percent
Fall quarter
Four-five-four calendar
Holiday quarter
Markdown
Markdown cancellation
Markdown dollars
Markdown price
Markup cancellation
Overbuying
Plan
Price change form
Reasons for markdowns
Retail
Retail sales
Special purchase
Spring quarter
Summer quarter

CHAPTER NINE
Closing Inventory

OBJECTIVES

After completing this chapter, you should be able to:

- Understand the importance of knowing the inventory level at all times and the causes and effects of shortage.
- Understand the importance of keeping accurate and precise records of all transactions when they affect stock levels.
- Understand the effect each different type of retail transaction has on the retail stock level.
- Apply these principles to a business.

CONCEPT

If you refer to Figure 9-1, you will see a reproduction of a simple profit statement. This document is probably the single most important document generated by any business. It is the record of the financial health of the organization. It is this document that determines who will be promoted, what department or branches get renovated, what areas will be expanded and funded, and, in fact, whether the company will stay in business. In this chapter, we will discuss inventory control, which affects the cost-of-goods-sold line on the profit statement.

Simple Profit or Loss	
Net sales	$100,000.00
Cost of inventory sold	$ 48,000.00
Cash discount	$ 3,000.00
Gross margin	$ 55,000.00
Operating expenses	$ 45,000.00
Profit	$ 10,000.00

Figure 9-1

There are five basic reasons to maintain an accurate accounting of inventory levels:

1. to maintain sufficient stock levels to support sales;
2. to take advantage of business opportunities;
3. to assess accurate tax and insurance levels;

4. to avoid needless markdowns;
5. to assist in the preparation of the profit-or-loss statement.

The first reason to maintain **sufficient stock levels** to support sales goes back to the idea of planning. When a marketing manager develops the seasonal plan, sales figures are estimated. In order to achieve the sales plan, the marketing manager must have enough stock to support the sales. Customers must be offered a sufficient number of styles, colors, and sizes in the right quantity to serve their needs and to provide a selection. Obviously, one item is not going to appeal to everyone. Because of the diversity in taste, the marketing manager must be prepared to service a variety of needs and desires. Also, merchandise takes a certain amount of time to be identified, counted, packed, shipped, received, and processed to be ready for sales (lead time). Additionally, no marketing manager is 100% right in figuring the customer's wants and needs. Mistakes are made (markdowns) and/or demands are underestimated (understocks). Therefore, it is imperative to have sufficient stock on hand to support sales and to cover the possibility of a greater acceptance than anticipated.

The second reason for an **accurate assessment of inventory levels** is to take advantage of unforeseen business opportunities. Once the marketing manager plans a sales level, a stock level is then derived that is sufficient to support the sales (the concept discussed previously). This stock level is based on:

1. historical performance for the merchandise type (frequency of purchase);
2. floor capacity for effective presentation;
3. how much merchandise is required to provide a selection without over-stocking.

Once the optimum stock level is established and the plan is approved, the marketing manager must live within the plan. By developing the plan, a commitment is made. In order to achieve goals, the restrictions must be adhered to as well. Therefore, it is essential to know at any given point where the stock level stands in relationship to the plan.

The third reason deals with the **taxes and insurance required** to protect the inventory. In every business, inventory costs money to maintain. Federal laws require taxes to be paid on inventory on hand. Business sense demands that the store carry sufficient insurance to protect against a major loss. Therefore, although the merchant must have sufficient stock on hand to support sales, paying exorbitant taxes and insurance premiums on merchandise that is not selling must be avoided.

The fourth reason to monitor stock levels is to **avoid needless markdowns.** Chapter Seven discussed the fact that markdowns lower the retail price on the goods, thereby forcing the marketing manager to make less money on each sale. If the marketing manager is over-stocked, money is tied up in goods that are not selling. This situation causes the marketing manager to:

1. be unable to reorder best-sellers;
2. have an appearance of "sameness" on the selling floor because of no open-to-buy;

3. be unable to display the merchandise properly (preventing a strong merchandise statement to the customer);
4. place the merchandise in the back stock room where it does not sell and may get either lost or damaged.

All this results in a loss of sales, an increase in markdowns, and, therefore, a loss in profit.

The last reason to maintain accurate records of inventory levels is to aid in the **preparation of profit statement.** By law, all businesses are required to prepare an income statement each year to determine tax levels. In order to do this, it is necessary to subtract all the firm's expenditures from its income to determine profit. Inventory is an expenditure (cost paid to the supplier, the freight involved in shipping the merchandise to the store, the taxes and insurance for the inventory on hand). Therefore, it is essential to know at all times what the stock investment is.

Clearly, because of the above reasons, it is to the marketing manager's advantage to know the status of the inventory. But, how is the stock level determined? One of the ways is to take a **physical inventory.** However this method is cumbersome and expensive. Therefore, marketing managers have developed a mathematical method of determining inventory levels. This method is called **book or statistical inventory.** By keeping tract of all transactions that affect the stock (receivings, sales, markdowns, claims, etc.), the marketing manager can estimate the dollar stock level. The word *estimate* is used because the marketing manager keeps track of the dollar amount of stock and not the actual physical amount. The dollar approach is the most realistic because it is physically impossible to watch every piece of merchandise in the business.

To work book inventory, the marketing manager has two alternatives: **cost or retail inventory.** In the retail industry, retail inventory is used because it is the easiest to figure on a daily basis. The task of maintaining a daily update at the retail level merely requires the marketing manager to keep track of the following:

1. beginning dollar stock—BOM (beginning of month);
2. dollar stock received—purchase or receipts;
3. dollar sales—retail gross sales;
4. dollar customer returns—customer returns and allowances;
5. dollar transfers in or out;
6. dollar merchandise returned to vendor—claims, RTV (return to vendor), RTM (return to manufacturer);
7. dollar price changes;
8. last year's shortage history.

By knowing the retail dollar amount of these transactions, the marketing manager can add or subtract the numbers involved based on their effect on stock levels and determine the established amount of stock on hand.

As you can see, keeping track of every retail transaction in itself can be a very cumbersome job. Therefore, when dealing with a large quantity of numbers, the simplest method is to combine them into groups. Marketing managers group the retail transaction into two categories: **total goods handled** (all transactions that increase the stock levels) and **total retail reductions** (all transactions that decrease the stock levels). After the subtotals of these two categories are calculated, they are subtracted from each other to derive the **book** or **statistical ending inventory (EOM).**

Once the marketing manager has figured out the estimated EOM, this number becomes the next month's BOM and the whole procedure is repeated. Therefore, this method provides the marketing manager a system to figure a perpetual inventory without ever taking a physical inventory.

Since this process is so simple, why do business people bother to take physical inventory? Basically there are two reasons. The first reason is that the law requires an annual physical inventory count. The second reason is to calculate the amount of inventory lost due to theft.

The process of comparing the physical inventory to the book inventory is called **reconciliation** and it involves a detailed review of all paperwork. Any errors on paper are adjusted to the statistical inventory. Once this procedure is done, the final statistical inventory is compared to the physical inventory. The difference between these two stock levels is called **overage** or **shortage**. *Shortage or overage is the unknown dollar amount the company lost or gained in inventory value.*

It is important for the marketing manager to know the amount of loss or gain in order to start the new year's book inventory with accurate numbers. Also, if a shortage has occurred, it is important to find the cause and take action to prevent it from happening in the future (e.g., change display methods or locations, reinstruct vendors in accounting procedures for the company). The main reasons for shortage and overage are bookwork errors (undiscovered during reconciliation) and theft (employee and customer). By determining which reason caused the shortage or overage, the marketing manager can take appropriate actions to improve next year's performance.

DEFINITIONS OF TERMS USED IN THIS CHAPTER

Beginning-of-month (BOM) — the dollar amount of stock existing at the start of the period; the value of the stock — part of total goods handled.

Book inventory — also know as statistical inventory. The dollar amount derived from accounting procedures involving all retail transactions during a period of time that affect dollar stock and applying the transactions to adjust the retail dollar stock of a physical inventory.

Claims (return to vendor) RTV/RTM — the dollar amount of merchandise sent back to the manufacturer for credit; a decrease to the stock—part of total retail reductions.

Customer returns and allowances — the dollar amount derived from a transaction in which the customer returns merchandise to the store for credit.

End-of-month (EOM) — also known as ending inventory. The dollar amount of stock existing at the end of the specified selling period (EOM for one month is the BOM for the next month).

Gross sales — the dollar amount of customer purchases before returns and allowances have been taken out.

Lead time — The amount of time needed to ship, unpack, mark, and deliver the goods to the selling floor.

Overage — the amount of money derived when the book inventory is lower than physical inventory.

Net sales — also known as income. The dollar amount of customer purchases after returns and allowances have been subtracted. Net sales reduce stock—part of total retail reductions.

Physical inventory — the actual dollar amount derived after physically counting all of the merchandise and extending retails to get a total.

Price changes: Additional markup, markdown, employee discount — repricing merchandise based on salability, cost fluctuation, and store policies. Additional markups (AMU) increase the stock—part of total goods handled. Markdowns (MD) and employee discount (ED) decrease the stock—part of total retail reductions.

Purchases (receipts) — the dollar amount of new merchandise received in a specific period of time; an increase to the stock—part of total goods handled.

Reconciliation — the act of investigating all discrepancies between the book and the physical inventory.

Simple profit statement — a report showing the basic profit factors that indicate the "financial health" of the company.

Shortage — the amount of money derived when the book inventory is greater than the physical inventory.

Shrinkage reserve — amount of money reduced from dollar stock level based on historical shortage performance—reduces the stock—part of total retail reductions.

Total goods handled — the total dollar amount of merchandise placed into the stock of the department during a specified period of time. It includes all transactions that increase the dollar value of the inventory.

Total retail reductions — the total dollar amount of merchandise removed from the stock investment existing in a department. It includes all transactions that reduce the dollar value of the inventory.

Transfer — the dollar amount of merchandise sent to or from another store. **Transfers in** increase the stock—part of total goods handled. **Transfers out** decrease the stock—part of total retail reductions.

NET SALES FORMULA

Gross sales – customer returns and allowances = net sales

****
BASIC RETAILING RULE #1

Retailers take a shortcut when dealing with numbers. Since so many numbers are large, retailers **abbreviate the numbers as follows: replace the first comma with a decimal point to express the number.** Therefore, $75,000.00 is expressed as $75.0; $35,500.00 is expressed as $35.5, and so forth. This abbreviation has absolutely no effect on the solution of the problem. It merely saves the retailer from entering all the zeroes on the calculator.

****

SAMPLE PROBLEM

Gross sales in June were $800.0. Customer returns and allowances were $40.0. What were the net sales?

STEP 1:   Formula:

Gross sales − customer returns and allowances = net sales

STEP 2:   Apply numbers to the formula.

$800.0 − $40.0 = $760.0

STEP 3:   Net sales = $760.0

IN-CLASS PRACTICE PROBLEMS

1. The furnishings department had gross sales of $680.0. Customer returns and allowances are $120.0. What are the net sales?

2. In June the gross sales for an offprice-speciality store were $50.0. In July, the owner noticed $10.0 reported in customer returns. What were the net sales?

3. The gross sales for the sporting goods department were $40.0. Customer returns for the same period were $5.0. What are the net sales?

4. A lingerie wholesaler had $60.0 in gross sales and $12.0 in returns. What were the net sales?

TOTAL GOODS HANDLED FORMULA

BOM + purchases + additional markups (AMU) + transfers in + markdown cancellations (MDC) = total goods handled (TGH)

● **SAMPLE PROBLEM**

Find the total goods handled for the following:

BOM	$600.0
Purchases	$100.0
Transfers in	$ 10.0
AMU	$ 15.0
MDC	$ 10.0

STEP 1:   TGH Formula:

BOM + purchases + AMU + MDC + transfers in + markdown cancellations = TGH

STEP 2:   Apply numbers to the formula.

$600.0 + $100.0 + $10.0 + $15.0 + $10.0 = $735.0

STEP 3:   Total goods handled = $735.0

●
IN-CLASS PRACTICE PROBLEMS

1. Figure the total goods handled for the following numbers:

BOM	$600.0
Transfers in	$210.0
AMU	$ 80.0
MDC	$100.0
Purchases	$100.0

2. Figure the total goods handled for the following numbers:

BOM	$80.0
Transfers in	$90.0
AMU	$10.0
MDC	$15.0
Purchases	$60.0

●

3. Figure the total goods handled for the following numbers:

BOM	$100.0
Transfers in	$ 10.0
AMU	$ 5.0
MDC	$ 2.0
Purchases	$ 60.0

FORMULA FOR TOTAL RETAIL REDUCTIONS

Net sales + claims + markdowns (MD) + employee discount + shrinkage reserve + transfers out + markup cancellations (MUC) = total retail reductions (TRR)

SAMPLE PROBLEM

Figure the total retail reductions for the following numbers:

Gross sales	$150.0
Customer returns and allowances	$ 20.0
MD	$ 10.0
MDC	$ 4.0
Employee discount	$ 2.0
Shortage reserve	$ 1.0
Transfers out	$ 1.0
Claims	$ 5.0

STEP 1:   Net sales formula:

Gross sales – customer returns and allowances = net sales

STEP 2:   Apply numbers to the formula.

$150.0 – $20.0 = $130.0

STEP 3:   Net sales = $130.0

STEP 4:   Total retail reductions formula:

Net sales + claims + MD + employee discount + MUC + transfers out + shortage + TRR

STEP 5:   Apply numbers to formula.

$130.0 + $10.0 + $4.0 + $2.0 + $1.0 + $1.0 + $5.0 = $153.0

STEP 6:   TRR = $153.0

IN-CLASS PRACTICE PROBLEMS

1. Figure the total retail reductions for the following numbers:

Gross sales	$200.0
Customer returns and allowances	$ 2.0
MD	$ 7.0
MUC	$ 1.0
Employee discount	$ 3.0
Shortage reserve	$ 2.0
Transfers out	$ 1.5
Claims	$ .5

2. Figure the total retail reductions for the following numbers:

Gross sales	$ 1,500.0
Customer returns and allowances	$ 15.6
MD	$ 206.0
MUC	$ 17.0
Employee discount	$ 5.0
Shortage reserve	$ 12.0
Claims	$ 15.0
Transfers out	$ 1.0

3. Figure the total retail reductions for the following numbers:

Gross sales	$ 1,600.0
Customer returns and allowances	$ 200.0
MD	$ 800.0
MUC	$ 900.0
Employee discount	$ 100.0
Shortage reserve	$ 50.0
Claims	$ 10.0
Transfers out	$ 15.0

CLOSING INVENTORY FORMULAS

Total goods handled – total retail reductions = EOM

****

BASIC CLOSING INVENTORY RULE #1:

Since this is a perpetual inventory, remember—EOM for one month is BOM for the next month.

****

SAMPLE PROBLEM

Figure the closing inventory for the following:

BOM	$ 50.0
Purchases	$ 25.0
Claims	$ 10.0
Transfers out	$ 5.0
Transfers in	$ 2.5
MD	$ 5.0
AMU	$ 2.5
Employee discount	$ 2.0
Gross sales	$ 10.0
Customer returns and allowances	$ 2.0

STEP 1:   Figure total goods handled.

BOM + purchases + transfers in + AMU = total goods handled

$50.0 + $25.0 + $2.5 + $2.5 = $80.0

STEP 2:   Total goods handled = $80.0

STEP 3:   Figure net sales.

Gross sales − customer returns & allowances = net sales

$10.0 − $2.0 = $8.0

STEP 4:   Figure total retail reductions formula.

Sales + markdowns + transfers out + claims + employee discount + shrinkage reserve = total reductions

$8.0 + $5.0 + $5.0 + $10.0 + $2.0 = $30.0

STEP 5:   Total retail reductions = $30.0

Figure closing inventory $80.0 − $30.0 = $50.0

STEP 6:   Closing inventory = $50.0

****

BASIC CLOSING INVENTORY RULE #2:

Always use the physical EOM inventory to start the next month's BOM if it is available.

****

IN-CLASS PRACTICE PROBLEMS

1. Beginning inventory for the men's knit department is $450.0. Purchases for that period were $700.0; net sales, $600.0; markdowns $60.0; claims $21.0; transfers out $25.0; and employee discounts $18.0. What is the statistical EOM? What is the BOM for the next month?

2. Using the following numbers, compute the EOM for the belt department for 1983:

   Physical inventory ending 1982 $ 75.0
   Purchases - 1983 $200.0
   Net sales - 1983 $150.0
   Claims - 1983 $ 20.0
   Markdowns - 1983 $ 5.0

3. The EOM book inventory for July is $75.0. The physical inventory for closing July is $72.5. What is the BOM for August?

4. What is the closing inventory for the following department numbers?

   BOM $ 75.0
   Net sales $ 80.0
   MD $ 6.0
   Purchases $ 50.0

FORMULA FOR OVERAGE AND SHORTAGE

Physical inventory − book inventory = overage or shortage

$$\frac{\text{part}}{\text{whole}} = \text{part \% (key)}$$

or

$$\frac{\$ \text{ overage or shortage}}{\text{cumulative net sales}} = \% \text{ overage or shortage (key)}$$

● **SAMPLE PROBLEM**

According to the first sample problem of this unit, book inventory for the period was $50.0 with net sales of $8.0. At the end of this period, a physical inventory was taken and amounted to $49.5. **What was the dollar and percent shortage or overage?**

STEP 1: Figure dollar shortage or overage.

Physical inventory − book inventory = shortage (−) or overage (+)

$49.5 − $50.0 = $.5

STEP 2: Dollar shortage = $.5

STEP 3: Figure % shortage.

$$\frac{\text{shortage dollars}}{\text{cumulative net sales}} = \% \text{ shortage (key)}$$

$$\frac{\$.5}{\$8.0} = x\% \text{ (key)}$$

Divide to get:

x = 6.3%

STEP 4: % shortage = 6.3%

IN-CLASS PRACTICE PROBLEMS

1. A departmental record of the ski department for the winter season shows the following numbers:

BOM	$ 225.0
Net sales	$ 200.0
Purchases	$ 150.0
Net MD	$ 8.5
Employee discount	$ 5.0
Claims	$ 1.0
Physical inventory	$ 154.5

   1. What was the book EOM?

2. What is the dollar and percent shortage or overage?

3. If the planned shortage was 6.8%, what is the dollar and percent shortage actual versus plan?

2. The annual figures for the women's lingerie department are as follows:

Net sales	$600.0
BOM	$150.0
MD & MUC	$ 15.0
AMU & MDC	$ 20.0
Transfer in	$135.0
Transfer out	$150.0
Employee discount	$ 6.0
Retail purchases	$650.0
Claims	$ 60.0
Closing physical	$130.0

1. What was the book EOM?

2. What is the dollar and percent shortage?

3. If the planned shortage was 3.0%, what is the dollar and percent difference versus plan?

3. Find the percent overage or shortage based on the following numbers:

Net sales	$ 60.0
Employee discount	$ 1.5
Retail purchase	$ 45.8
Opening inventory	$130.0
Net MD	$ 7.2
Claims	$ 12.8
Closing physical	$104.8

4. Net sales for the shoe department last year were $565.0. Closing book was $185.0 while closing physical was $168.0. What is the shortage percent?

5. Based on the following numbers, what is the EOM, dollar and percent shortage?

BOM	$ 1,500.0
Purchases	$ 600.0
Net sales	$ 750.0
Claims	$ 200.0
MD	$ 150.7
AMU	$ 80.9
MDC	$ 30.8
MUC	$ 20.5
Transfer in	$ 116.9
Transfer out	$ 218.4
Employee discount	$ 9.6
Closing physical inventory	$ 900.8

HOMEWORK

1. Figure the retail perpetual book inventory for the following department.

	FEB	MAR	APR	MAY	JUNE	JULY
BOM	$500.6					
Purchases	$100.0	$160.0	$ 90.0	$140.0	$400.0	$150.0
Transfer in	$ 5.0	$ 17.0	$ 12.3	$ 50.0	$ 15.0	$ 0.0
Additional Markup	$ 17.6	$ 15.0	$ 7.0	$ 25.0	$ 17.6	$ 28.0
Total Goods Handled						
Net sales	$125.0	$100.0	$ 75.0	$100.0	$300.0	$180.0
Employee Discount	$ 1.6	$ 4.0	$ 1.5	$ 5.0	$ 18.0	$ 7.2
Markdowns	$ 17.0	$ 2.0	$ .3	$ 1.6	$ 11.3	$ 16.2
Total Retail Reductions						
Book Inventory						

2. In this department, if the EOM physical inventory in May was $700.0, what was the dollar and percentage shortage/overage? (BEFORE figuring the percentage, remember to use the cumulative net sales. If it took 4 months to generate this shortage, then you must use 4 months' net sales to figure the percent shortage.)

3. Using the numbers in the form, if the physical closing inventory for June was $700.0, what is the dollar or percent shortage?

4. Using the numbers on the form again, if the July physical inventory shows a shortage of 7.0%, what is the dollar shortage? dollar physical EOM?

5. On the following form, figure the dollar closing inventory.

	FEB	MAR	APR	MAY	JUNE	JULY
BOM	$563.0					
Purchases	$100.0	$110.0	$120.0	$300.0	$100.0	$ 50.0
Transfer in	$ 7.0	$ 6.0	$ 4.0	$ 5.3	$ 5.0	$ 15.0
Total goods handled						
Gross sales	$ 60.0	$ 70.0	$ 90.0	$270.0	$150.0	$100.0
Customer returns	$ 5.0	$ 1.4	$ 5.0	$ 2.7	$ 5.0	$ 6.0
Net Sales						
Markdowns	$ 10.0	$ 2.1	$ 15.0	$ 8.0	$ 6.0	$ 7.0
Employee discounts	$ 3.0	$ .7	$ 1.7	$ 2.7	$ 1.4	$ 21.0
Total retail reductions						
EOM						

6. Using the numbers of the form, what is the percent and dollar overage/shortages in the following instances:

   1. If physical EOM February = $600.0?

   2. If physical EOM April = $600.0?

   3. If physical EOM June = $500.0?

   4. If percent shrinkage EOM July = 3.0%, what is the dollar shrinkage and EOM July physical?

CHALLENGER

1. **Figure perpetual inventory.**

	FEB	MAR	APR	MAY	JUNE
BOM					$700.0
Purchases	$100.0	$110.0	$120.0	$300.0	$100.0
Transfers in	$ 7.0	$ 6.0	$ 4.0	$ 5.3	$ 5.0
AMU	$ 10.0	$ 2.7	$ 35.0	$ 2.7	$ 70.0
Total goods handled					
Gross sales		$ 70.0	$ 90.0		$150.0
Customer returns and allowances	$ 1.8	$ 3.2		$ 2.9	$ 6.0
Net sales	$ 58.2		$ 85.7	$267.1	
Markdown	$ 10.0	$ 2.1	$ 15.0	$ 8.0	$ 6.0
Employee discount	$ 3.0	$ .7	$ 1.7	$ 2.7	$ 1.4
Total retail reductions					
Book inventory					

2. **Using the above numbers, figure the dollar and percent of shrinkage based on the following figures:**
   1. If physical EOM March $600.0
   2. If physical EOM May $700.0
   3. If physical EOM June $695.6

3. **What is the June physical EOM and dollar shrinkage if the June percent shrinkage is 2.4%?**

CHAPTER NINE: SUMMARY

The procedures involved in reconciliation of book and physical inventories are mathematically very simple. However, the implications of poor inventory control are far-reaching throughout the business. Overstocking, theft, insufficient stock, and paperwork errors all lead to unnecessary, controllable loss. To ensure the maximum performance in the business, the marketing manager must keep updated constantly regarding the actual stock levels versus planned stock levels.

KEY TERMS

Beginning inventory (BOM)
Book or statistical inventory
Claims/returns to vendor (RTV, RTM)
Customer returns and allowances
Ending inventory (EOM)
Gross sales
Lead time
Overage
Net sales
Physical inventory
Price changes - additional markup, markdown, and employee discount
Purchases (receipts)
Reconciliation
Simple profit statement
Shortage
Shrinkage reserve
Total goods handled
Total retail reduction
Transfers in or out

PART FOUR: PROFIT

CHAPTER TEN
Skeletal Profit and Loss Statements

OBJECTIVES

After completing this chapter, you should be able to:

- Understand the concepts and terminology of profit and loss.
- Understand the importance of developing a skeletal profit and loss statement.
- Understand the mechanics involved in calculating skeletal profit and loss.
- Apply the mechanics to a business situation.

CONCEPT

Simple Profit or Loss	
Net Sales	$ 100.0
Cost of Inventory Sold	$ 48.0
Cash Discount	$ 3.0
Gross Margin	$ 55.0
Operating Expenses	$ 45.0
Profit	$ 10.0

Figure 10-1

The desire for profits is the reason individuals create businesses. The profit and loss statement is considered the business owner's "report card." A profit statement, therefore, is a measurement of how well the business is planned, organized, and controlled.

To understand a profit and loss statement (also known as an operating statement), it is crucial to understand the meaning of each line. The first line of the profit statement is **net sales**. Net sales is the number that is used as a base to measure performance because it is in the income of a retail business. This number represents the total amount of customer purchases. It indicates how well the owner has merchandised the business to reflect the target customer's wants and needs and how well the merchandise has been priced.

The next line on the profit statement is the **cost of inventory sold** (also known as **cost of goods or cost of merchandise sold**). This number relates to the profit and loss statement because the cost of the merchandise must be subtracted from the income. Marketing managers figure cost only on the sold merchandise so that the figures on the statement are consistent—sales refers to the income generated from the retail merchandise sold; cost of inventory refers to the money spent for the merchandise sold. This number is determined by how well the owner has negotiated with the vendor on the terms of the sale.

Cash discount (discussed in Chapter 5), because it is a plus to the marketing manager, is added back into the difference between the net sales and the cost of goods sold.

Gross margin is a very important number to the business because it represents the money made from the sales. Every line above the gross margin is controlled by the company—net sales are generated because the right goods were purchased and priced correctly; cost of goods sold is dependent upon negotiating the best deal possible with the vendor; and cash discount is the result of negotiating the terms of the sale and following up to make sure the bills are paid on time. Since the company has complete control of all the elements involved in calculating gross margin, the performance on this line is a common form of evaluation. Raises and salaries can depend on a good performance on this line.

Once the gross margin is determined, all the **overhead (expenses)** of running the business are subtracted from gross margin dollars to derive profit. Many expenses are not controllable (such as utility rates). However, some expenses are controllable. It is the owner's job to make sure that controllable expenses (salaries, advertising) are kept in line with the profit goals of the business. Once the profit dollars are derived, profit is calculated also as a percent of net sales. This provides a measurement of performance (e.g., a 3.0% profit means that for every one dollar in sales, the company makes three cents in profit).

As discussed before, profit is the reason for being in business. Profit is used for two purposes: first, to produce capital for reinvestment; and second, to provide money to return to investors as dividends. Both of these purposes are essential for the continued growth and health of the business. Stagnation in the current economy can only spell eventual disaster. A company that is breaking even today will go under tomorrow due to inflation, rising cost of overhead, and competition. By mastering the concepts that generate profit, the company's success is assured—*and so is yours!*

DEFINITIONS OF TERMS USED IN THIS CHAPTER

Advertising — a paid presentation in a media by an identified sponsor.

Capital for reinvestment — the amount of money put back into the business for expansion or refurbishing.

Cash discount — the amount of money taken off the invoice as an incentive for prompt payment.

Cost of inventory sold — also known as cost of goods or merchandise sold. The dollar amount of money paid to get the merchandise sold ready for sale.

Dividends — the amount of money returned to the investors because the profits of the business were good.

Expenses — also know as operating expenses. The amount of money charged for upkeep and promotion of the business and facility; salaries, advertising, and buying. Overhead.

Gross margin — the money the buyer earns after paying for the cost of goods and before expenses are taken out.

Gross sales — the dollar amount of customer purchases before returns and allowances have been taken out.

Net sales — the dollar amount derived from customer purchases after returns and allowances have been taken out.

Operating statement — a report showing the profit performance for a business for a specific period of time.

Profit — also known as operating profit. The money the buyer earns after expenses are subtracted from the gross margin dollars.

Profit percent — also known as operating profit percent. The relationship between operating profit dollars and net sales expressed as part of 100.

Returns and allowances — the dollar amount derived from a transaction in which the customer returns the merchandise to the store for credit.

Salaries — the amount of money spent for staff remuneration.

GROSS MARGIN FORMULA

Net sales − cost of goods sold + cash discount = gross margin

SAMPLE PROBLEM

Figure the gross margin based on the following numbers:

Gross sales	$150.0
Customer returns and allowances	$ 30.0
Cost of goods sold	$ 70.9
Cash discount	$ .6

STEP 1:   Net sales formula:

                     Gross sales – customer returns and allowances = net sales

STEP 2:   Apply numbers to the formula.

                     $150.0 – $ 30.0 = $120.0

STEP 3:   Net sales = $120.0

STEP 4:   Gross margin formula:

                     Net sales – cost of goods sold + cash discount = gross margin

STEP 5:   Apply numbers to the formula.

                     $120.0 – $70.9 + $.6 = $49.7

STEP 6:   Gross margin = $49.7

IN-CLASS PRACTICE PROBLEMS

1. Figure the gross margin for the following:

Gross sales	$180.0
Customer returns and allowances	$ 80.0
Cost of goods sold	$ 94.0
Cash discount	$ 5.0

2. Figure the gross margin for the following:

Gross sales	$600.0
Customer returns and allowances	$ 60.0
Cost of goods sold	$340.0
Cash discount	$ 6.0

3. Figure the gross margin for the following:

Gross sales	$100.0
Customer returns and allowances	$ 20.0
Cost of goods sold	$ 63.0
Cash discount	$ 5.0

PROFIT FACTOR PERCENT FORMULA

$$\frac{\text{profit factor}}{\text{net sales}} = \text{profit factor \% (key)}$$

SAMPLE PROBLEMS

1. **Using the gross margin formula and the percentage formula, fill in the following gross margin statement.**

	Dollars	Percent
Net sales	$100.0	_____
Cost of goods sold	_____	51.3%
Cash discount	$ 5.0	
Gross margin	_____	_____

STEP A: Profit factor formula:

$$\frac{\text{profit factor}}{\text{net sales}} = \text{profit factor \% (key)}$$

STEP B: Apply numbers to the formula:

$$\frac{\$100.0}{\$100.0} = 100.0\%$$

STEP C: Net sales % = 100.0%

STEP D: Profit factor formula:

$$\frac{\text{profit factor}}{\text{net sales}} = \text{profit factor \% (key)}$$

STEP E: Apply numbers to the formula.

$$\frac{x}{\$100.0} = 51.3\%$$

STEP F: Cost of goods sold dollars = $51.3

STEP G: Gross margin formula:

Net sales – cost of goods sold + cash discount = gross margin

STEP H: Apply numbers to the formula.

$100.0 – $51.3 + $5.0 =$ 53.7

STEP I: Gross margin $ = $53.7

STEP J: Profit factor formula:

$$\frac{\text{profit factor}}{\text{net sales}} = \text{profit factor \% (key)}$$

STEP K: Apply numbers to the formula.

$$\frac{\$53.7}{\$100.0} = 53.7\%$$

STEP L: Gross margin % = 53.7%

Recap of Information

	Dollars	Percent
Net sales	$100.0	100.0%
Cost of goods sold	$ 51.3	51.3%
Cash discount	$ 5.0	
Gross margin	$ 53.7	53.7%

2. **Using the gross margin and the percent formula, fill in the following gross margin statement.**

	Dollars	Percent
Net sales	_____	100.0%
Cost of goods sold	$ 56.0	61.8%
Cash discount	$ 1.0	
Gross margin	_____	_____

STEP A:　　　　　Profit factor formula:

$$\frac{\text{profit factor}}{\text{net sales}} = \text{profit factor \% (key)}$$

STEP B:　　　　　Apply numbers to the formula.

To calculate net sales

$$\frac{\text{cost of goods sold}}{\text{net sales}} = \text{cost of goods sold \% (key)}$$

$$\frac{\$56.0}{x} = 61.0\%$$

Net sales = $91.8

STEP C:　　　　　Net sales = $91.8

STEP D:　　　　　Gross margin formula:

Net sales − cost of goods sold + cash discount = gross margin

STEP E:　　　　　Apply numbers to the formula.

Net sales	$ 91.8
− Cost of goods sold	$ 56.0
+ Cash discount	$ 1.0
Gross margin	$ 36.8

STEP F:　　　　　Gross margin $ = $36.8

STEP G: Profit factor formula:

$$\frac{\text{profit factor}}{\text{net sales}} = \text{profit factor \% (key)}$$

STEP H: Apply numbers to the formula.

$$\frac{\text{gross margin}}{\text{net sales}} = \text{gross margin \% (key)}$$

$$\frac{\$36.8}{\$91.8} = 40.1\%$$

STEP I: Gross margin % = 40.1%

IN-CLASS PRACTICE PROBLEMS

	Dollars	Percent
1. Net sales	$ 10.0	_____
Cost of goods sold	_____	58.3%
Cash discount	$ 1.0	
Gross margin	_____	_____

	Dollars	Percent
2. Net sales	_____	100.0%
Cost of goods sold	$110.0	58.9%
Cash discount	$ 5.6	
Gross margin	_____	_____

	Dollars	Percent
3. Net sales	_____	100.0%
Cost of goods sold	$100.0	55.6%
Cash discount	$ 6.0	
Gross margin	_____	_____

	Dollars	Percent
4. Net sales	$ 22.0	100.0%
Cost of goods sold	_____	48.6%
Cash discount	$ .1	
Gross margin	_____	_____

	Dollars	Percent
5. Net sales	_____	_____
Cost of goods sold	$ 33.0	51.3%
Cash discount	$ 5.5	
Gross margin	_____	_____

PROFIT/LOSS FORMULA

Gross margin – expenses = profit/loss

SAMPLE PROBLEM

---

1. **A buyer's gross sales were $150.0 with customer returns of $2.5. With the following figures, complete the operating profit dollars and percent to net sales.**

Cost of goods sold	$ 31.2
Cash discount	$ 2.5
Operating expenses	(35% of net sales)

    STEP A: Figure net sales.

    Gross sales – customer returns = net sales

    $150.0 – $2.5 = $147.5

    STEP B: Net sales = $147.5

STEP C: Profit factor formula:

$$\frac{\text{profit factor}}{\text{net sales}} = \text{profit factor \% (key)}$$

STEP D: Apply numbers to the formula.

1. $\dfrac{\text{net sales}}{\text{net sales}}$ = net sales % (key)

   $$\frac{\$147.5}{\$147.5} = 100\%$$

   Net sales % = 100.0%

2. Cost of goods sold percent formula:

   $$\frac{\text{Cost of goods sold}}{\text{Net sales}} = \text{cost of goods sold \% (key)}$$

   $$\frac{\$\,31.2}{\$147.5} = \text{x\% (key)}$$

   Divide to get 21.2%.

   Cost of goods sold % = 21.2%

STEP E: Gross margin formula:

Net sales − cost of goods sold + cash discount = gross margin

STEP F: Apply numbers to the formula.

$147.5 − $31.2 + $2.5 = $118.8

Gross margin = $118.8

STEP G: Profit factor formula:

$$\frac{\text{profit factor}}{\text{net sales}} = \text{profit factor \% (key)}$$

STEP H: Apply numbers to the formula.

$$\frac{\text{gross margin \$}}{\text{net sales}} = \text{gross margin \% (key)}$$

$$\frac{\$118.8}{\$147.5} = \text{x\% (key)}$$

Divide to get:

x = 80.5%

STEP I: Gross margin $ = 80.5%

STEP J: Profit factor formula:

$$\frac{\text{profit factor}}{\text{net sales}} = \text{profit factor \% (key)}$$

STEP K: Apply numbers to the formula.

$$\frac{\text{operating expenses \$}}{\text{net sales}} = \text{operating expenses \% (key)}$$

Apply numbers to the formula.

$$\frac{x}{\$147.5} = 35.0\% \text{ (key)}$$

Multiply to get:

x = $51.6

STEP L: Operating expenses = $51.6

STEP M: Profit formula:

Gross margin − operating expenses = operating profit

STEP N: Apply numbers to the formula.

$118.8 − $51.6 = x

STEP O: Operating profit = $67.2

STEP P: Profit factor formula:

$$\frac{\text{profit factor}}{\text{net sales}} = \text{profit factor \% (key)}$$

STEP Q: Apply numbers to the formula.

$$\frac{\text{operating profit}}{\text{net sales}} = \text{operating profit \% (key)}$$

$$\frac{\$67.2}{\$147.5} = x\% \text{ (key)}$$

Divide to get: x = 45.5%

STEP R: Operating profit % = 45.5%

STEP S: Summary:

	Dollars	Percent
Net sales	$147.5	100.0%
Cost of goods sold	$ 31.2	21.2%
Cash discount	$ 2.5	
Gross margin	$118.8	80.5%
Operating expenses	$ 51.6	35.0%
Operating profit	$ 67.2	45.5%

IN-CLASS PRACTICE PROBLEMS

1. The departmental figures for the young activewear area this year are as follows:

   Cost of goods sold $207.3
   Net sales $506.0
   Cash discount $ 4.1
   Expenses   (45.0% of net sales)

   a. Calculate cost of goods percent.

   b. Find the operating expense dollars.

   c. Determine the profit or loss dollars and percent.

2. If the total operating expenses are $79.6 and the gross margin is $59.2, what is the operating profit or loss?

3. If the operating profit dollars are $8.0 and the percentage is 12.1%, what were the net sales?

4. For the housewares department, gross sales are $151.8, cost of goods sold is $75.1, customer returns and allowances are $7.9, and cash discount is $2.1, What is the gross margin dollars and percent?

5. Make a profit or loss statement for the following department:

    Cost of goods sold $350.0
    Operating expenses $190.8
    Net sales $550.0
    Cash discount $ 5.0

238

Chapter Ten: Skeletal Profit and Loss Statements

HOMEWORK

1. Calculate the net sales for the following departmental numbers:

   Gross margin $ 75.8
   Net profit   1.3%
   Operating expenses $ 70.3

2. If the furniture department has a loss of $4.1 for the fall season and its gross margin was $47.8, what must the dollar amount of expenses be?

3. Find the gross margin dollars and percent for the shoe department:

   Cost of goods sold $110.0
   Gross sales $279.6
   Customer returns and allowances $ 1.7
   Cash discount $ 13.0

4. The gross margin dollars for the men's clothing department was $205.0. Operating expenses amounted to $185.0 and net profit was 6.0% of net sales. What were the total net sales dollars for this department?

5. Determine the net sales for the auto parts store:

   Operating expenses $ 79.6
   Gross margin $ 75.6
   Net loss   1.0%

6. The loss for a handbag wholesaler was $7.8. This is 6.0% of the business's net sales. What are the sales dollars?

7. Find the gross margin for dollars and percent for the accessories department:

Cost of goods sold	$450.0
Gross sales	$757.9
Customer returns	$ 78.3
Cash discounts	$ 9.8

8. Make up the annual profit and loss statement for the children's department, providing both dollars and percentage figures for all profit elements.

Cost of goods sold	$115.0
Cash discount	$ 5.7
Gross sales	$276.9
Customer returns	$ 13.0
Expenses	(46.0% of net sales)

9. For its first year in business, a limousine service's annual figures show the following:

Gross margin	$ 12.7
Operating expenses	$ 11.4
Profit	3.1%

    Determine the net sales dollars.

10. Prepare a dollar and percentage profit and loss statement for the housewares department.

   Net sales $565.4
   Cost of goods sold $204.0
   Profit   8.1%
   (no cash discount in this department)

11. Create the profit and loss statement in the case goods department where the sales were $4,567.0, cost of goods were 53.8%, and the operating expenses were $2,160.0.

242

CHALLENGERS

Fill in the following worksheet.

WORKSHEET

1. Operating Statement. Fill in the monthly numbers.

	FEB	MAR	APR	MAY	JUNE	JULY	TOTAL
Gross sales	$21.5		$16.4		$12.6		
Customer returns	$ .2	$ .3	$ .4	$ .2	$ 1.2	$ 1.9	
Net sales		$27.7		$13.0		$17.5	
Cost of goods	$14.1	$15.6	$ 7.1	$ 8.0	$ 5.0	$ 8.3	
Cash discounts	$ .3	$ .1	$ .5	$ .8	$ 1.1	$ .4	
Gross margin %							

2. Use gross margin numbers and form below to figure operating profit.

	FEB	MAR	APR	MAY	JUNE	JULY	TOTAL
Gross margin							
Total expenses	$ 6.0	$12.0	$ 6.1	$ 5.0	$ 7.5	$ 8.0	
Operating profit $							
Operating profit %							

3. Find cumulative numbers for the six-month period in space provided.

CHAPTER TEN: SUMMARY

Profit and loss statements are necessary controlling factors in business. By knowing the key terms, concepts, and calculations involved, the business owner can effectively plan, organize, and control the business to ensure its survival and ultimate success.

KEY TERMS TO REVIEW

Advertising
Capital for reinvestment
Cash discount
Cost of inventory (merchandise, goods) sold
Dividends
Expenses
Gross margin
Gross sales
Net sales
Operating statement
Profit—operating profit
Profit percent
Returns and allowances
Salaries

CHAPTER ELEVEN
Detailed Operating Statement

OBJECTIVES

After completing this chapter, you should be able to:

- Understand how markup, markdown, and closing inventory are used in calculating profit and loss.
- Understand that each of these factors affects profit and loss dollars for a business.
- Understand the mechanics involved in developing a detailed profit and loss statement.
- Apply these mechanics to a business situation.

CONCEPT

As stated before, the profit and loss statement is the single most important document in a business. The previous chapter demonstrated the techniques involved in calculating a skeletal profit and loss statement. However, the skeletal statement does not provide a true picture of the interrelationship between the profit factors and the ultimate performance of the company.

In this chapter, we will start at the beginning, "building" a detailed profit and loss statement. This will involve the following steps:

1. Calculating total retail reductions;
2. Determining cumulative markup percent;
3. Computing the cost of goods sold;
4. Figuring gross margin dollars and percent;
5. Calculating expense dollars;
6. Deriving the resulting profit or loss dollars and percent.

The first step, calculating total retail reductions, illustrates the impact of markdowns, employee discounts, and shrinkage. The combining of these factors provides the owner with a graphic demonstration of the negative impact markdowns, employee discount, and shrinkage have on the business. The larger these numbers are, the smaller the ultimate profit will be. Through controlling the levels of these factors, the owner protects the profit performance of the business.

The second step, determining cumulative markup percent, provides the owner with a true picture of the value of the total stock. This picture is derived because cumulative markup is the relationship between markup dollars and retail of the purchases plus the existing stock.

The third step, computing the cost of goods sold, encompasses all expenditures involved in getting the goods ready to sell. These expenditures include:

1. Cost of merchandise (terms of the sale, markup of goods);

2. Value of inventory (closing inventory procedures);
3. Freight charges;
4. Total retail reductions (markdowns, employee discounts, shrinkage, net sales);
5. Workroom

From the above list, it is evident that all concepts and procedures covered in this book are now being put into use to calculate cost of goods sold—a major profit factor. Cost of goods sold is subtracted from net sales to determine gross profit.

The fourth step, figuring gross margin, includes adding cash discount dollars to the gross profit dollars. Gross margin, therefore, is the amount of money the business makes before expenses are subtracted.

The fifth step, computing expense dollars, involves looking at all the overhead incurred by the business. Expenses are grouped into two categories—direct (variable) and indirect (fixed). The most common form of identifying expenses is to group them into expenses centers. The *Financial Operating Results* (FOR), published by the National Retail Merchants Association, lists the following expense centers:

Direct:

1. Sales promotion (includes management, advertising, media, special events, visual presentation);
2. Personnel (includes management, payroll, training, employee service {medical}, supplementary benefits);
3. Merchandising (includes management, buying, travel, merchandise control);
4. Distribution/selling support (includes receiving, storage, distribution, management, marking, shuttle services, selling supervision, customer services, selling support services, central wrapping and packing, deliver).

Indirect:

1. Real estate (includes rent, taxes, insurance, fixtures, equipment rental);
2. Company management (includes executive office, branch management, internal auditing, legal and consumer activities);
3. Accounting and management information (includes sales audit, accounts payable, data processing);
4. Credit and accounts receivable (management, collections, bill adjustment);
5. Services and operations management (security, telephone and communication, utilities, housekeeping, maintenance and repairs)

Direct or **variable expenses** are the dollars charged to the business over which the owner has control. These charges usually reflect an increase in sales (e.g., the more sales made by the business, the more staff hours required). **Indirect** or **fixed expenses** are those charges that exist whether or not the business makes any sales (e.g., the rent has to be paid for the entire year, regardless of whether the company is operating or not). Once the direct and indirect expense dollars are computed, they are added together to get total expense dollars.

The last step, deriving the profit or loss, involves subtracting the total expense dollars from the gross margin dollars. The resulting number is the profit or loss for the business.

With the exception of cash discount (which is figured as a percent of cost purchases), all other profit factors are calculated as a percent of net sales. By using net sales as a base, the marketing manager can identify the size of each factor in relationship to a single number. He or she can then take these percentages and compare them to the numbers in the *FOR* for his or her business type to see if any are out of line. Through identifying problem areas in the business, the owner can take corrective action (e.g., improve shortage performance through more accurate accounting policies, negotiate for better prices or terms of sale with suppliers).

DEFINITION OF TERMS USED IN THIS CHAPTER

Closing inventory procedures — method described in previous chapter which determines the cost of goods sold.

Cumulative markup percent — the relationship between markup dollars and retail derived when purchases and existing stock are combined.

Expenses — dollar amount paid in overhead by the business

Freight — dollar amount paid for transportation charges.

Gross profit — dollar amount derived when the cost of goods sold is subtracted from the income.

Purchases — the dollar amount of merchandise received in a specific period of time.

Shrinkage reserve — the dollar amount of money taken off the stock value determined by historical shortage performance.

Workroom — any charges incurred by the business to prepare, repair, or alter the merchandise.

TOTAL RETAIL REDUCTIONS FORMULA

OPERATING STATEMENT WORKSHEET		
	Retail	% of Net Sales
1. Net sales	Given	100.0%
2. Net markdowns	% × Net Sales	$ - Net Sales
3. Employee discount	% × Net Sales	$ – Net Sales
4. Shrinkage reserve	% × Net Sales	$ – Net Sales
5. Total retail reductions	1 + 2 + 3 + 4	2 + 3 + 4

SAMPLE PROBLEM

The owner of the Royal Duffy Coffee and Tea Shoppe was calculating the total retail reductions from the following information:

Net sales $ 330.0

Net markdowns   1.3%

Employee discount $ 3.3

Shrinkage Reserve   1.2%

STEP 1:   Net markdown formula:

$$\frac{\text{markdown \$}}{\text{retail}} = \text{markdown \%}$$

STEP 2:   Apply numbers to the formula.

$$\frac{x}{\$330.0} = 1.3\%$$

STEP 3:   Multiply to get:

net markdowns = $ 4.3

STEP 4:   Employee discount formula:

$$\frac{\text{employee discount \$}}{\text{retail}} = \text{employee discount \%}$$

STEP 5:   Apply numbers to the formula.

$$\frac{\$ 3.3}{\$330.0} = x\%$$

STEP 6:   Divide to get:

employee discount % = 1.0%

STEP 7:   Shrinkage reserve formula:

$$\frac{\text{shrinkage reserve \$}}{\text{retail}} = \text{shrinkage reserve \%}$$

STEP 8:   Apply numbers to the formula.

$$\frac{x}{\$330.0} = 1.2\%$$

STEP 9:   Multiply to get:

shrinkage reserve $ = \$4.0$

STEP 10:   Total retail reduction formula:

Net sales + markdowns + employee discount + shrinkage = total retail reduction

STEP 11:   Apply numbers to the formula.

$\$330.0 + \$4.3 + \$3.3 + \$4.0 = \$341.6$

STEP 12:   Total retail reduction percent formula:

Markdowns % + employee discount % + shrinkage % = total retail reduction %

STEP 13:   Apply numbers to the formula.

$1.3\% + 1.0\% + 1.2\% = 3.5\%$

OPERATING STATEMENT WORKSHEET		
	Retail	% of Net Sales
1. Net sales	$ 330.0	100.0%
2. Net markdowns	$ 4.3	1.3%
3. Employee discount	$ 3.3	1.0%
4. Shrinkage reserve	$ 4.0	1.2%
5. Total retail reductions	$ 341.6	3.5%

IN-CLASS PRACTICE PROBLEMS

1. Fill in the following chart.

OPERATING STATEMENT WORKSHEET		
	Retail	% of Net Sales
1. Net sales	$ 75.0	
2. Net markdowns		5.0%
3. Employee discount		3.0%
4. Shrinkage reserve .		2.0%
5. Total retail reductions		

2. Fill in the following chart.

OPERATING STATEMENT WORKSHEET		
	Retail	% of Net Sales
1. Net sales	$1,450.0	
2. Net markdowns	$ 120.0	
3. Employee discount		.7%
4. Shrinkage reserve	$ 75.0	
5. Total retail reductions		

3. Fill in the following chart.

OPERATING STATEMENT WORKSHEET		
	Retail	% of Net Sales
1. Net sales	$1,045.0	
2. Net markdowns		4.0%
3. Employee discount	$ 6.3	
4. Shrinkage reserve		9.0%
5. Total retail reductions		

4. Fill in the following chart.

OPERATING STATEMENT WORKSHEET		
	Retail	% of Net Sales
1. Net sales		
2. Net markdowns	$ 12.0	3.0%
3. Employee discount	$ 5.0	
4. Shrinkage reserve	$ 40.0	
5. Total retail reductions		

CUMULATIVE MARKUP CALCULATIONS

OPERATING STATEMENT WORKSHEET		
	Retail	% of Net Sales
1. Net sales		
2. Net markdowns		
3. Employee discount		
4. Shrinkage reserve		
5. Total retail reductions		

	Cost	Retail	Markup %
6. Beginning stock	comp. × retail	BOM	markup % on stock
7. Net purchases	comp. × retail	purchase	markup % on purchases
8. Total stock	6 + 7	6 + 7	$\dfrac{\text{retail–cost}}{\text{retail}}$
9. Ending stock	comp. × retail	8 - 5	cumulative markup %

comp. = complement

SAMPLE PROBLEM

Continuing the profit and loss statement of Royal Duffy Coffee and Tea Shoppe, the owner determines her stock numbers to be as follows:

	Retail	Markup %
BOM	$ 100.0	45.0%
Purchases	$ 450.0	47.0%

Fill out the numbers through line 9.

STEP 1:   Place numbers in the appropriate boxes.

OPERATING STATEMENT WORKSHEET		
	Retail	% of Net Sales
1. Net sales	$ 330.0	100.0%
2. Net markdowns	$ 4.3	1.3%
3. Employee discount	$ 3.3	1.0%
4. Shrinkage reserve	$ 4.0	1.2%
5. Total retail reductions	$ 341.6	3.5%

	Cost	Retail	Markup %
6. Beginning stock		$100.0	45.0%
7. Net purchases		$450.0	47.0%
8. Total stock			
9. Ending stock			

STEP 2:   Markup % complement formula:

$$\frac{\text{cost}}{\text{retail}} = \text{markup \% complement}$$

STEP 3:   Apply numbers to the formula.

Line 6:

$$\frac{x}{\$100} = 55.0\% \ (100\% - 45\% = 55.\%)$$

Multiply to get:

$\$100.0 \times 55\% = \$55.0$

Line 7:

$$\frac{x}{\$450} = 53.0\% \ (100\% - 47\% = 53\%)$$

Multiply to get:

$\$450.0 \times 53\% = \$238.5$

STEP 4:   Add lines 6 and 7 at cost.

$\$55.0 + \$238.5 = \$293.5$

STEP 5:   Add lines 6 + 7 at retail.

$\$100.0 + \$450.0 = \$550.0$

STEP 6:   Markup percent formula:

$$\frac{\overset{\text{(retail} - \text{cost)}}{\text{markup \$}}}{\text{retail}} = \text{markup } \%$$

STEP 7:   Apply numbers to the fomula.

$\$550.0 - \$239.5 = \$256.5$

$$\frac{\$256.5}{\$550.0} = 46.6\%$$

STEP 8:   Cumulative markup % = 46.6%

STEP 9:   Copy cumulative markup % to line 9.

STEP 10:   Subtract total retail reductions (line 5) from total stock (line 8).

$\$550.0 - \$341.6 = \$208.4$

STEP 11:   Markup percent complement formula:

$$\frac{cost}{retail} = \text{markup \% complement}$$

STEP 12:   Apply numbers to the formula.

$$\frac{x}{\$208.4} = 53.4\% \ (100\% - 46.6\% = 53.4\%)$$

Multiply to get:

$$\$208.4 \times 53.4\% = \$111.3$$

Recap:

OPERATING STATEMENT WORKSHEET		
	Retail	% of Net Sales
1 Net sales	$ 330.0	100.0%
2. Net markdowns	$ 4.3	1.3%
3. Employee discount	$ 3.3	1.0%
4. Shrinkage reserve	$ 4.0	1.2%
5. Total retail reductions	$ 341.6	3.5%

	Cost	Retail	Markup %
6. Beginning stock	$ 55.0	$100.0	45.0%
7. Net purchases	$238.5	$450.0	47.0%
8. Total stock	$293.5	$550.0	46.6%
9. Ending stock	$111.3	$208.4	46.6%

IN-CLASS PRACTICE PROBLEMS

1. Fill in the following chart.

OPERATING STATEMENT WORKSHEET		
	Retail	% of Net Sales
1. Net sales	$ 191.4	
2. Net markdowns		8.1%
3. Employee discount		2.3%
4. Shrinkage reserve	$ 16.0	
5. Total retail reductions		

	Cost	Retail	Markup %
6. Beginning stock		$378.2	50.0%
7. Net purchases		$ 96.5	52.0%
8. Total stock			
9. Ending stock			

2. Fill in the following chart.

OPERATING STATEMENT WORKSHEET		
	Retail	% of Net Sales
1. Net sales	$ 196.6	
2. Net markdowns	$ 8.0	
3. Employee discount		2.3%
4. Shrinkage reserve		1.8%
5. Total retail reductions		

	Cost	Retail	Markup %
6. Beginning stock		$287.8	48.0%
7. Net purchases		$143.3	50.0%
8. Total stock			
9. Ending stock			

3. Fill in the following chart.

OPERATING STATEMENT WORKSHEET		
	Retail	% of Net Sales
1. Net sales	$ 85.0	
2. Net markdown		2.0%
3. Employee discount		1.5%
4. Shrinkage reserve		.9%
5. Total retail reductions		

	Cost	Retail	Markup %
6. Beginning stock		$190.0	56.8%
7. Net purchases		$100.0	57.0%
8. Total stock			
9. Ending stock			

COST OF GOODS SOLD FORMULA

OPERATING STATEMENT WORKSHEET			
		Retail	% of Net Sales
1. Net sales			
2. Net markdowns			
3. Employee discount			
4. Shrinkage reserve			
5. Total retail reductions			
	Cost	Retail	Markup %
6. Beginning stock			
7. Net purchases			
8. Total stock			
9. Ending stock			
	Cost		% of Net Sales
10. Total stock cost	Line 8 cost		
11. Freight	% × sales		% of net sales
12. Total cost	10 + 11		
13. Ending stock cost	line 9 cost		
14. Workroom	% × sales		% of net sales
15. Cost of goods sold	12 − 13 + 14		% of net sales

● SAMPLE PROBLEM

Calculate the cost of goods sold line for the Royal Duffy Coffee and Tea Shoppe using the following information:

Freight   1.0% of net sales
Workroom   .1% of net sales

STEP 1:   Copy line 8 at cost to line 10.

STEP 2:   Freight dollars formula:

$$\frac{\text{freight dollars}}{\text{net sales}} = \text{freight \%}$$

STEP 3:   Apply numbers to the formula.

$$\frac{x}{\$330.0} = 1.0\%$$

Multiply to get:

$\$330.0 \times 1.0\% = \$3.3$

STEP 4:   Freight dollars = $3.3

STEP 5:   Add line 10 plus line 11.

$\$293.5 + \$3.3 = \$296.8$

STEP 6:   Copy line 9 at cost to line 13.

STEP 7:   Workroom formula:

$$\frac{\text{workroom \$}}{\text{net sales}} = \text{workroom \%}$$

STEP 8:   Apply numbers to the formula.

$$\frac{x}{\$330.0} = .1\%$$

Multiply to get:

$\$330.0 \times .1\% = \$.3$

STEP 9:   Workroom dollars = $.3

STEP 10:   Line 12 − line 13 + line 14 = cost of goods sold (line 15)

STEP 11:   Apply numbers to the formula.

$296.8 − $111.3 + $.3 = $185.8

STEP 12:   Cost of goods sold = $185.8

STEP 13:   Cost of goods sold formula:

$$\frac{\text{cost of goods \$}}{\text{net sales}} = \text{cost of goods \%}$$

STEP 14:   Apply numbers to the formula.

$$\frac{\$185.8}{\$330.0} = x\%$$

Divide to get:

x = 56.3%

STEP 15:   Cost of goods sold percent = 56.3%

OPERATING STATEMENT WORKSHEET			
		Retail	% of Net Sales
1. Net sales		$ 330.0	
2. Net markdowns		$ 4.3	1.3%
3. Employee discount		$ 3.3	1.0%
4. Shrinkage reserve		$ 4.0	1.2%
5. Total retail reductions		$ 341.6	3.5%
	Cost	Retail	Markup %
6. Beginning stock	$ 55.0	$100.0	45.0%
7. Net purchases	$238.5	$450.0	47.0%
8. Total stock	$293.5	$550.0	46.6%
9. Ending stock	$111.3	$208.4	46.6%
	Cost		% of Net Sales
10. Total stock cost	$293.5		
11. Freight	$ 3.3		1.0%
12. Total cost	$296.8		
13. Ending stock cost	$111.3		
14. Workroom	$ .3		.1%
15. Cost of goods sold	$185.8		56.3%

IN-CLASS PRACTICE PROBLEMS

1. Fill in the following chart.

OPERATING STATEMENT WORKSHEET			
		Retail	% of Net Sales
1. Net sales		$1,000.0	
2. Net markdowns			15.0%
3. Employee discount			4.5%
4. Shrinkage reserve			6.0%
5. Total retail reductions			
	Cost	Retail	Markup %
6. Beginning stock		$ 1,500.0	51.0%
7. Net purchases		$ 1,200.0	51.2%
8. Total stock			
9. Ending stock			
	Cost		% of Net Sales
10. Total stock cost			
11. Freight			3.0%
12. Total cost			
13. Ending stock cost			
14. Workroom			1.5%
15. Cost of goods sold			

2. Fill in the following chart.

OPERATING STATEMENT WORKSHEET			
		Retail	% of Net Sales
1. Net sales		$ 30.7	
2. Net markdowns		$ 1.2	
3. Employee discount		$ .5	
4. Shrinkage reserve		$ .1	
5. Total retail reductions			
	Cost	Retail	Markup %
6. Beginning stock		$ 70.0	54.7%
7. Net purchases		$ 45.0	55.2%
8. Total stock			
9. Ending stock			
	Cost		% of Net Sales
10. Total stock cost			
11. Freight			0%
12. Total cost			
13. Ending stock cost			
14. Workroom			0%
15. Cost of goods sold			

GROSS MARGIN

OPERATING STATEMENT WORKSHEET			
		Retail	% of Net Sales
1. Net sales			
2. Net markdowns			
3. Employee discount			
4. Shrinkage reserve			
5. Total retail reductions			
	Cost	Retail	Markup %
6. Beginning stock			
7. Net purchases			
8. Total stock			
9. Ending stock			
	Cost		% of net sales
10. Total stock cost			
11. Freight			
12. Total cost			
13. Ending stock cost			
14. Workroom			
15. Cost of goods sold			
16. Gross profit	1 − 15		% of net sales
17. Cash discount	% × 7 cost		% of cost purch.
18. Gross margin	(16 + 17)		% of net sales

SAMPLE PROBLEM

Complete the profit and loss statement to the gross margin line for the Royal Duffy Coffee and Tea Shoppe using a cash discount of 2.0%.

STEP 1:   Subtract line 15 from line 1.

$330.0 − $185.8 = $144.2

STEP 2:   Determine cash discount dollars:

$$\frac{\text{cash discount \$}}{\text{cost purchases}} = \text{cash discount \%}$$

STEP 3:   Apply numbers to the formula.

$$\frac{x}{\$238.5} = 2.0\%$$

Multiply to get:

$238.5 × 2.0% = $4.8

STEP 4:   Add line 16 plus line 17.

$144.2 + $4.8 = $149.0

STEP 6:   Gross margin % formula

$$\frac{\text{gross margin \$}}{\text{net sales}} = \text{gross margin \%}$$

STEP 7:   Apply numbers to the formula.

$$\frac{\$149.0}{\$330.0} = x$$

Divide to get:

x = 45.2%

OPERATING STATEMENT WORKSHEET			
		Retail	% of Net Sales
1. Net sales		$ 330.0	
2. Net markdowns		$ 4.3	1.3%
3. Employee discount		$ 3.3	1.0%
4. Shrinkage reserve		$ 4.0	1.2%
5. Total retail reductions		$ 341.6	3.5%
	Cost	Retail	Markup %
6. Beginning stock	$ 55.0	$100.0	45.0%
7. Net purchases	$238.5	$450.0	47.0%
8. Total stock	$293.5	$550.0	46.6%
9. Ending stock	$111.3	$208.4	46.6%
	Cost		% of Net Sales
10. Total stock cost	$293.5		
11. Freight	$ 3.3		1.0%
12. Total cost	$296.8		
13. Ending stock cost	$111.3		
14. Workroom	$ .3		.1%
15. Cost of goods sold	$185.8		56.3%
16. Gross profit	$144.2		43.7%
17. Cash discount	$ 4.8		% of cost purch. 2.0%
18. Gross margin	$149.0		45.2%

IN-CLASS PRACTICE PROBLEM

OPERATING STATEMENT WORKSHEET		
	Retail	% of Net Sales
1. Net sales	$ 58.3	
2. Net markdowns	$ .6	
3. Employee discount		1.4%
4. Shrinkage reserve		.6%
5. Total retail reductions		

	Cost	Retail	Markup %
6. Beginning stock		$193.0	56.8%
7. Net purchases		$175.0	57.0%
8. Total stock			
9. Ending stock			

	Cost		% of Net Sales
10. Total stock cost			
11. Freight			4.0%
12. Total cost			
13. Ending stock cost			
14. Workroom			.1%
15. Cost of goods sold			
16. Gross profit			
17. Cash discount			% of cost purch. 8.0%
18. Gross margin			% of net sales

OPERATING STATEMENT WORKSHEET			
		Retail	% of Net Sales
1. Net sales		$ 175.0	
2. Net markdowns			4.0%
3. Employee discount			2.0%
4. Shrinkage reserve			.3%
5. Total retail reductions			
	Cost	Retail	Markup %
6. Beginning stock		$300.0	51.0%
7. Net Purchases		$190.0	51.3%
8. Total stock			
9. Ending stock			
	Cost		% of Net Sales
10. Total stock cost			
11. Freight			.5%
12. Total cost			
13. Ending stock cost			
14. Workroom			.1%
15. Cost of goods sold			
16. Gross profit			
17. Cash discount			% of cost purch. 3.0%
18. Gross margin			% of net sales

EXPENSE FORMULA

OPERATING STATEMENT WORKSHEET			
		Retail	% of Net Sales
1. Net sales			
2. Net markdowns			
3. Employee discount			
4. Shrinkage reserve			
5. Total retail reduction			
	Cost	Retail	Markup %
6. Beginning stock			
7. Net purchases			
8. Total stock			
9. Ending stock			
	Cost		% of Net Sales
10. Total stock cost			
11. Freight			
12. Total cost			
13. Ending stock cost			
14. Workroom			
15. Cost of goods sold			
16. Gross profit			
17. Cash discount			% of cost purch.
18. Gross margin			% of net sales
EXPENSES:			% of Net Sales
19. Sales promotion	$\% \times$ sales		% of net sales
20. Personnel	$\% \times$ sales		% of net sales
21. Merchandising	$\% \times$ sales		% of net sales
22. Distribution/support	$\% \times$ sales		% of net sales
23. Total indirect	$\% \times$ sales		% of net sales
24. Total expenses	$19 + 20 + 21 + 22 + 23$		$19 + 20 + 21 + 22 + 23$
25. Total profit	$18 - 24$		% of net sales

SAMPLE PROBLEM

Complete the profit and loss statement for the Royal Duffy Coffee and Tea Shoppe using the following expense numbers:

Sales promotion	3.0%
Personnel	20.0%
Merchandising	8.0%
Distribution/support	2.0%
Indirect	8.5%

STEP 1:   Calculate the expense dollars.

$$\frac{\text{expense \$}}{\text{net sales}} = \text{expense \%}$$

STEP 2:   Apply numbers to the formula.

Sales promotion:

$$\frac{x}{\$330.0} = 3.0\%$$

Multiply to get:

x = $9.9

Personnel:

$$\frac{x}{\$330.0} = 20.0\%$$

Multiply to get:

x = $66.0

Merchandising:

$$\frac{x}{\$330.0} = 8.0\%$$

Multiply to get:

x = $26.4

Distribution and support:

$$\frac{x}{\$330.0} = 2.0\%$$

Multiply to get:

x = $6.6

Indirect:

$$\frac{x}{\$330.0} = 8.5\%$$

Multiply to get:

x = $28.1

STEP 3:   Total expense dollars:

$9.9 + $66.0 + $26.4 + $6.6 + $28.1 = $137.0

STEP 4:   Total expense percentage:

3.0% + 20.0% + 8.0% + 2.0% + 8.5% = 41.5%

STEP 5:   Subtract total expenses from gross margin (line 18).

$149.0 − $137.0 = $12.0

STEP 6:   Profit formula:

$$\frac{\text{profit \$}}{\text{net sales}} = \text{profit \%}$$

STEP 7:   Apply numbers to the formula.

$$\frac{\$12.0}{\$330.0} = x\%$$

Divide to get:

x = 3.6%

STEP 8:   Profit % = 3.6%

(See completed profit and loss on next page.)

OPERATING STATEMENT WORKSHEET			
		Retail	% of Net Sales
1. Net sales		$330.0	
2. Net markdowns		$ 4.3	1.3%
3. Employee discount		$ 3.3	1.0%
4. Shrinkage reserve		$ 4.0	1.2%
5. Total retail reductions		$341.6	3.5%
	Cost	Retail	Markup %
6. Beginning stock	$ 55.0	$100.0	45.0%
7. Net purchases	$238.5	$450.0	47.0%
8. Total stock	$293.5	$550.0	46.6%
9. Ending stock	$111.3	$208.4	46.6
	Cost		% of Net Sales
10. Total stock cost	$293.5		
11. Freight	$ 3.3		1.0%
12. Total cost	$296.8		
13. Ending stock cost	$111.3		
14. Workroom	$ .3		.1%
15. Cost of goods sold	$185.8		56.3%
16. Gross profit	$144.2		43.7%
17. Cash discount	$ 4.8		2% of cost purch.
18. Gross margin	$149.0		45.2%
EXPENSES:			% of Net Sales
19. Sales promotion	$ 9.9		3.0%
20. Personnel	$ 66.0		20.0%
21. Merchandising	$ 26.4		8.0%
22. Distribution/support	$ 6.6		2.0%
23. Total indirect	$ 28.1		8.5%
24. Total expenses	$137.0		41.5%
25. Total profit	$ 12.0		3.6%

HOMEWORK

Complete the operating statements on pp. 274-275.

OPERATING STATEMENT WORKSHEET			
		Retail	% to Net Sales
1. Net sales		$158.0	
2. Net markdowns			4.0%
3. Employee discount		$ 5.0	
4. Shrinkage reserve			2.1%
5. Total retail reductions			
	Cost	Retail	Markup %
6. Beginning stock		$325.0	53.8%
7. Net purchases		$200.0	54.0%
8. Total stock			
9. Ending stock			
	Cost		% to Net Sales
10. Total stock cost			
11. Freight			1.0%
12. Total cost			
13. Ending stock cost			
14. Workroom			.2%
15. Cost of goods sold			
16. Gross profit			
17. Cash discount			3% of cost purch.
18. Gross margin			% of net sales
EXPENSES:			% of Net Sales
19. Sales promotion			4.5%
20. Personnel			15.0%
21. Merchandising			7.0%
22. Distribution/support			3.5%
23. Total indirect			5.5%
24. Total expenses			
25. Total profit			

OPERATING STATEMENT WORKSHEET			
		Retail	% of Net Sales
1. Net sales		$250.0	
2. Net markdowns			.7%
3. Employee discount		$ 2.5	
4. Shrinkage reserve		$ 4.0	
5. Total retail reductions			
	Cost	Retail	Markup %
6. Beginning stock		$352.4	53.9%
7. Net purchases		$300.0	54.0%
8. Total stock			
9. Ending stock			
	Cost		% of Net Sales
10. Total stock cost			
11. Freight			1.0%
12. Total cost			
13. Ending stock cost			
14. Workroom			2.0%
15. Cost of goods sold			
16. Gross profit			
17. Cash discount			
18. Gross margin			% of net sales
EXPENSES:			% of Net Sales
19. Sales promotion			4.5%
20. Personnel			15.0%
21. Merchandising			7.0%
22. Distribution/support			3.5%
23. Total indirect			5.5%
24. Total expenses			
25. Total profit			

CHALLENGER

On the following operating statement, do the cumulative numbers for these two months.

NOTE: Use the *first* profit and loss BOM (do not add them together). Add sales, markdowns, employee discount, shortage, receipts, freight, workroom, and expense dollars for both months to get your numbers. *Do not add* percentages. *Do not add* stock numbers; follow the procedures outlined in this unit!

OPERATING STATEMENT WORKSHEET			
		Retail	% of Net Sales
1. Net sales			
2. Net markdowns			
3. Employee discount			
4. Shrinkage reserve			
5. Total retail reductions			
	Cost	Retail	Markup %
6. Beginning stock			
7. Net purchases			
8. Total stock			
9. Ending stock			
	Cost		% of Net Sales
10. Total stock cost			
11. Freight			
12. Total cost			
13. Ending stock cost			
14. Workroom			
15. Cost of goods sold			
16. Gross profit			
17. Cash discount			
18. Gross margin			
EXPENSES:			% of Net Sales
19. Sales promotion			
20. Personnel			
21. Merchandising			
22. Distribution/support			
23. Total indirect			
24. Total expenses			
25. Total profit			

CHAPTER ELEVEN: SUMMARY

Although the calculations involved in profit and loss statements are simple when taken by themselves, the interrelationships of the factors make the application seem complex. However, by learning each of the calculations separately (each are applications found in Units 1-10 in this book) and understanding the concept of each application, the profit and loss statement becomes less confusing. The profit and loss shows dramatically how each transaction in the business impacts the final performance of the company.

KEY TERMS

Closing inventory procedures
Cumulative markup percent
Expenses
Freight
Gross profit
Purchases
Shrinkage reserve
Workroom

CHAPTER TWELVE
Final Review

PURPOSE

This chapter deals with a review of the merchandise math concepts in this book.

EQUATIONS

PART AND WHOLE RELATIONSHIP

Percentage Increase/Decrease:

New amount + or − $ increase/decrease = old amount

Old amount + or − $ increase/decrease = new amount

Old amount − new amount = $ increase/decrease

Markup:

Markup $ + cost = retail

Retail − markup $ = cost

Retail − cost = markup $

Markdown:

Markdown price + markdown $ = retail

Retail − markdown $ = markdown price

Retail − markdown price = markdown $

Employee Discount:

Discount price + discount $ = retail

Retail − discount $ = discount price

Retail − discount price = discount $

BASIC EQUATIONS

$$\frac{\text{Part}}{\text{Whole}} = \% \text{ (key)}$$

Percentage increase/decrease:

$$\frac{\$ \text{ Difference}}{\text{Old amount}} = \% \text{ increase/decrease (key)}$$

Markup:

$$\frac{\text{Markup } \$}{\text{Retail}} = \text{markup } \% \text{ (key)}$$

Markdown:

$$\frac{\text{Markdown } \$}{\text{Retail}} = \text{markdown } \% \text{ (key)}$$

Employee Discount:

$$\frac{\text{Discount } \$}{\text{Retail}} = \text{discount } \% \text{ (key)}$$

SPECIAL EQUATIONS
(never to be used when both right-hand side elements are known!)

Percentage increase/decrease:

$$\frac{\text{New amount}}{\text{Old amount}} = \begin{array}{c} \% \text{ increase} + 100\% \\ \text{OR} \\ \% \text{ decrease} - 100\% \end{array}$$

Markup:

$$\frac{\text{Cost}}{\text{Retail}} = \text{markup } \% \text{ complement (key)}$$

Markdown:

$$\frac{\text{Markdown price}}{\text{Retail}} = \text{markdown } \% \text{ complement (key)}$$

Employee Discount:

$$\frac{\text{Discount price}}{\text{Retail}} = \text{discount } \% \text{ complement (key)}$$

TO FIND MARKUP % OF GROUPS

1. Extend quantity × cost per each style and retail to get style extensions.
2. Add cost extensions to get total cost.
3. Add retail extensions to get total retail.
4. Total retail – total cost = total markup dollars.
5. $\dfrac{\text{Total markup \$}}{\text{Total retail}}$ = initial markup % (key)

TO FIND MARKDOWN % OF GROUPS

1. Extend quantity × retail per each style and markdown dollars per style to get style extensions.
2. Add extensions of retail to get total retail.
3. Add extensions of markdown dollars to get total markdown dollars.
4. $\dfrac{\text{Total markdown dollars}}{\text{Total retail}}$ = total markdown %

TO FIND AVERAGE MARKUP %

1. Find markup percent complement for each markup given in problem.
2. Find total cost and/or retail using markup percent or markup percent complement formula.
3. Find already-bought cost and/or retail using markup percent or markup percent complement formula.
4. Subtract **Total** columns *only* to get balance-to-buy cost and/or retail.
5. Find markup percent for balance if needed.
6. Find unit cost or retail if requested in problem.
7. Find balance-to-buy retail.
8. Find balance-to-buy markup %.
9. Find average cost or retail per unit if requested.

****

SPECIAL RULES FOR AVERAGING

1. If a retail is set in a problem, it remains set throughout the problem.
2. If there is a quantity listed in the problem, extend to totals to work the problem. (*Never* work at the unit level).

****

FINDING CLOSING INVENTORY

Gross sales − customer returns & allowances = net sales

BOM + purchases + additional markup + markdown cancellations + transfers in = total goods handled

Net sales + markdowns + employee discount + shortage + transfers out + claims + markup cancellations = total retail reduction

Basic closing inventory formula:

total goods handled − total retail reductions = closing inventory

Finding dollars and percent overage/shortage:

physical inventory − book inventory = $ overage/shortage

$\dfrac{\text{\$ overage/shortage}}{\text{cumulative net sales}}$ = % shortage/overage

****

SPECIAL RULES CLOSING INVENTORY

1. End of month for one month becomes beginning of month for the next month.
2. Only retail transactions are involved in closing inventory.
3. Use cumulative net sales for entire period during which the shortage or overage was generated.

****

DOLLAR PROFIT AND LOSS STATEMENT

Basic formula:

```
   net sales
−  cost of goods sold
+  cash discount
   gross margin
−  operating expenses
   operating profit or loss
```

PERCENTAGES FOR PROFIT AND LOSS STATEMENTS

Profit factor = Profit or loss % (key)

● **DEFINITIONS**

Study all definitions given to date in the chapters.

IN-CLASS PRACTICE PROBLEMS

1. The blouse buyer purchases some short-sleeved tailored blouses that cost $165.00 per dozen. She plans to take a 54.3% markup. What are the retail and markup dollars per unit?

2. The coat buyer purchases two styles of raincoats that cost $38.50 each. She decides to retail them at $85.00 each. What are the markup percent and markup dollars?

3. The men's furnishings buyer purchases a closeout of socks costing $18.00 per dozen. If he adds $2.00 per pair in markup dollars, what are the retail and markup percent?

4. The hosiery buyer purchases slippers, having $12.00 in markup dollars, giving her a 57.9% markup. What are the retail and cost on these slippers?

5. A jacket retails for $58.00, having a 55.3% markup. What are the cost and markup dollars?

6. A mohair coat retailing at $1,075.00 has markup dollars of $576.00. What are the cost and markup percent?

7. The sportswear buyer is shown a group of cotton coordinates she is considering purchasing for her department. She chooses the following styles:

Style #	Description	Qty.	Cost	Retail	Markup $	Markup %
5106	Culottes	28	$12.00	$30.00		
6106	Sweaters	28	$25.00		$30.00	
8106	T-Shirts	59	$ 9.00			51.4%
9106	Slacks	36		$26.00	$16.00	
9206	Shorts	28		$15.00		55.6%
2106	Jackets	28			$39.00	53.2%

What are the total cost, retail, and markup percent for this purchase? (Use purchase order on p. 294.)

8. The shoe buyer purchases some sandals for a pre-season sale. She purchases the following:

Style #	Description	Qty.	Cost	Retail	Markup $	Markup %
0016	White	160	$15.00			51.8%
0017	Beige	197		$17.50		50.2%
0018	Tan	216		$30.99		51.1%

What are the total cost, retail, and markup percent? (Use purchase order on p. 295.)

9. The lingerie buyer plans purchases of $800.0 at retail at a 54.1% markup. Her purchases-to-date are $300.0 at cost with a 51.0% markup. What are her remaining purchases? (Use form on p. 296.)

10. A buyer plans to purchase 2,000 units of accessories for a $10.99 sale. She must maintain an overall 51.2% markup on her purchases. Her first purchase of 500 units cost $6.00 each. Her second purchase of 750 units cost $5.50 each. What are the remaining numbers? If she buys the remaining units from one vendor, what should the unit cost be to make her plan? (Use form on p. 296.)

11. The dress buyer plans to spend $1,500.0 for the fall season at a 53.6% markup. She has already spent $535.0 at cost at a 52.8% markup. What are the remaining numbers? (Use form on p. 296.)

12. The china buyer plans to purchase 600 units for a new store opening. Her planned retail stock is $750.0 at a 52.4% markup. She has purchased 400 units totaling $300.00 cost at a 52.0% markup. What is her remaining open-to-buy? If she purchases all the remaining units at the same cost and retails them all the same, what are the average cost and retail per unit? (Use form on p. 297.)

13. The shirt buyer marks down a long-sleeved plaid shirt from $35.00 to $21.99. What are the markdown percent and markdown dollars?

14. The lingerie buyer has silk camisoles at $25.00 retail that she reduces 25.0%. What are the markdown price and markdown dollars?

15. The junior buyer advertises two-piece dresses at $31.99, which was a 33.3% markdown from the retail. What were the retail and markdown dollars?

16. The active-sportswear buyer has some poor-selling jogging suits that she must clear to make room for her new goods. On the first style, she marks it down to $21.99, taking $25.00 off the retail. For the second style, she took $20.01 off the retail, offering the customer a 41.0% savings. The third style, originally retailing at $55.00, she reduced 36.2%. What are all the pricing factors involved?

17. Using the information derived in problem 16, the buyer received her markdown counts from her store. On the first style, she had 162 units, on the second style she had 53 units, and on the third style she had 201 units. What are her planned markdown dollars for the group? What is the total markdown percent of this group? (Use price change form on p. 298.)

18. A buyer's sales plan call for $150,000.00 sales in the month of June with a 16% markdown plan. She takes $20,000.00 in markdown dollars for the month. What is her percent? Will she make her plan?

19. A buyer's retail sales for the spring season were $1,365,00.00. She took $85,000.00 worth of markdowns. If her markdown plan was 15%, can she make her plan? What is the difference between dollars and percent?

20. A buyer takes the following markdowns for December: 62 units at $16.00 retail, taking 31.2% off, 38 units taking $14.00 off the original retail, making the new retail $25.99; and 51 units taking $23.00 off the original retail for 61.4% markdown. What were dollars and percent for this group? (Use price change form on p. 299.)

21. An employee is entitled to a 25.5% discount on all her purchases in the store. She purchases a silk dress that retails for $162.00. What was her discount price?

22. Mary purchases a skirt for $24.00, a sweater for $16.50, and a pair of shoes for $19.99. If on these purchases she receives a 20.0% discount, what were the original retails for each of these items?

23. If an employee receives a 12.0% discount on all purchases, what is the original retail and discount price for an item on which she gets $17.00 off?

24. An executive is entitled to a 32.5% discount. He purchases the following for his wife's anniversary presents: a dress for $62.00, a pair of shoes on which he saves $16.00, and a coat that originally retailed for $158.00. What are all the price factors of the above items? The dollar discount? The total original retail on the entire purchase? The total discount price the executive paid for the purchase, not including sales tax?

25. Opening inventory for the bra department is $200.0. Purchases for the period were $600.0. Net sales were $500.0. Price changes were $50.0. Claims were $80.0 and employee discounts were $5.0. What is the EOM for the next period? the BOM for the next?

26. Using the following numbers, compute the EOM for the hat department.

Physical inventory	$ 80.0
Purchases	$250.0
Net sales	$175.0
Claims	$ 25.0
Markdowns	$ 10.0

27. The annual figures for the Christmas department were as follows:

BOM	$100.0
Sales	$200.0
Purchases	$150.0
MD	$ 25.0
Employee Discount	$ 5.0
Claims	$ 20.0
Physical inventory	$ 0

    a. What is the closing book inventory?
    b. What is the shortage/overage in dollars and percent?
    c. If the planned shortage was .5%, what are the dollars and percent difference.

28. The annual figures for the small-leather goods department are as follows:

Net sales	$500.0
BOM	$ 50.0
MD & MDC	$ 5.0
AMU & MDC	$ 10.0
Transfers out	$ 35.0
Transfers in	$ 50.0
Employee discount	$ 5.0
Retail purchases	$550.0
Claims	$ 50.0
Closing physical inventory	$ 30.0

a. What is the book EOM?
b. What is the dollar and percent shortage or overage?
c. If the planned shortage was 1%, what is the dollar and percent shortage or overage difference actual versus plan?

29.

	$	%
Net sales	$600.0	100.0%
Cost of goods sold	_____	43.2%
Cash discount	$ 20.7	
Gross margin	_____	
Operating expenses	_____	25.8%
Operating profit	_____	_____

30.

	$	%
Net sales	_____	100.0%
Cost of goods sold	$258.0	$40.2%
Cash discounts	$ 18.0	
Gross margin	_____	
Operating expenses	_____	31.8%
Operating profit	_____	_____

31. If total operating expenses are $85.0 and the gross margin is $81.3, what is the operating profit or loss?

32. If the operating profit dollars are $51.0 and the percentage is 9.8%, what were the net sales?

33. If the gross margin percent was 49.8% and the operating loss was 3%, what was the operating expense percent?

34. Make a profit and loss statement based on the following numbers, providing both dollars and percent for all profit elements.

	$	%
Cost of goods sold	$114.6	_____
Cash discount	$ 8.0	
Gross sales	$300.0	_____
Customer returns	$ 18.0	_____
Expenses	(38.6% of net sales)	

35. Prepare a dollar and percentage profit and loss statement for the bath linen department.

	$	%
Net sales	$500.0	_____
Cost of goods sold	$235.0	_____
Cash discount	$ 6.0	
Expenses	$180.0	_____

36. Prepare a dollar and percent profit and loss statement based on the following numbers.

	$	%
Gross sales	$500.0	_____
Customer returns	$ 50.0	_____
Expenses	$185.0	_____
Cost of goods sold	$262.0	_____

PURCHASE ORDER

STORE NAME: _____

DEPT: _____

ORDER DATE: _____

DO NOT SHIP BEFORE: _____

CANCEL IF NOT RECD: _____

VENDOR: _____

ADDRESS: _____

FREIGHT ALLOWANCE: _____

FOB PT: _____

SHIP VIA: _____

TERMS: _____ % EOM

NO: _____

CLASS	DESCRIPTION	STYLE	SIZE	COLOR	TOTAL UNITS	COST EA	COST TOT	RET EA	RET TOT	MU%	MU$
TOTALS											

BUYER'S SIGNATURE: _____

PURCHASE ORDER

NO: _____

STORE NAME: _____

DEPT: _____ VENDOR: _____ FREIGHT ALLOWANCE: _____

ORDER DATE: _____ ADDRESS: _____ FOB PT: _____

DO NOT SHIP BEFORE: _____ SHIP VIA: _____

CANCEL IF NOT RECD: _____ TERMS: _____ % EOM

CLASS	DESCRIPTION	STYLE	SIZE	COLOR	TOTAL UNITS	COST EA	COST TOT	RET EA	RET TOT	MU%	MU$
		TOTALS									

BUYER'S SIGNATURE: _____

	Quantity	Unit Cost	Cost Ext.	Unit Retail	Retail Ext.	Markup %
Total Needed						
Already Bought						
Balance-to-Buy						

	Quantity	Unit Cost	Cost Ext.	Unit Retail	Retail Ext.	Markup %
Total Needed						
Already Bought						
Balance-to-Buy						

	Quantity	Unit Cost	Cost Ext.	Unit Retail	Retail Ext.	Markup %
Total Needed						
Already Bought						
Balance-to-Buy						

	Quantity	Unit Cost	Cost Ext.	Unit Retail	Retail Ext.	Markup %
Total Needed						
Already Bought						
Balance-to-Buy						

PRICE CHANGE

NO : _____
DATE: _____
STORE: _____
DEPT: _____

Indicate type of price change with an X.
Use separate sheet for each type of change.

X _____ Markdown
_____ Markdown Cancellation
_____ Markup
_____ Markup Cancellation

CLASS	MFG	DESCRIPTION	UNITS	OLD RET	NEW RET	DIFFERENCE	EXTENSION	MD%
						TOTAL		

SIGNATURE: _____

PRICE CHANGE

Indicate type of price change with an X.
Use separate sheet for each type of change.

X   Markdown   _____

       Markdown Cancellation   _____

       Markup   _____

       Markup Cancellation   _____

NO : _____
DATE: _____
STORE: _____
DEPT: _____

CLASS	MFG	DESCRIPTION	UNITS	OLD RET	NEW RET	DIFFERENCE	EXTENSION	MD%
						TOTAL		

SIGNATURE: _____

FIRST HALF REVIEW ANSWER SHEET

Final Review

1. $\dfrac{C}{R}$ = comp

   $165 \div 12 = \$13.75$ cost per unit

   $\$30.09 - \$13.75 = \$16.34$

   $100\% - 54.3\% = 45.7\%$ complement

   $\dfrac{\$13.75}{45.7}$ = % (key)

   Retail = \$30.09
   Markup \$ = \$16.34

2. $\dfrac{MU\ \$}{R}$ = MU %

   $\$85.00 - \$38.50 = \$46.50$
   $\quad$ R $\ -\ $ C $\ =$ MU \$

   $\dfrac{\$46.50}{\$85.00} = 54.705882\%$

   Markup \$ = \$46.50
   Markup % = 54.7%

3. $\dfrac{MU\ \$}{R}$ = MU %

   $\$18 \div 12 = \$1.50$

   $\$1.50 + \$2.00 = \$3.50$
   $\ $ C $\ +\ $ MU $\ =$ R

   $\dfrac{\$2.00}{\$3.50} = 57.1\%$

   Retail = \$3.50
   Markup % = 57.1%

4. $\dfrac{MU\ \$}{R}$ = MU %

   $\$20.73 - \$12.00 = \$8.73$

   $\dfrac{\$12.00}{x} = 57.9\% = \$20.725388$

   Retail = \$20.73
   C = \$8.73

5. $\dfrac{MU\$}{R}$ = MU %

   $\dfrac{x}{\$58.00} = 55.3\% = \$32.074$

   $\$58.00 - \$32.07 = \$25.93$

   Markup \$ = \$32.07
   C = \$25.93

6. $\dfrac{MU\ \$}{R}$ = MU %

   $\$1,075.00 - \$576.00 = \$499.00$
   $\quad$ R $\quad - $ MU\$ $\ =\quad$ C

   $\dfrac{\$\,576.00}{\$1,075.00} = 53.581395\%$

   C = \$499.00
   Markup % = 53.6%

7. See purchase order on p. 307.

8. See purchase order on p. 308.

9. See averaging form on p. 309.

10. See averaging form on p. 309.

11. See averaging form on p. 309.

12. See averaging form on p. 310.

13. $\dfrac{MD\ \$}{R} = MD\ \%$

$35.00 - \$21.99 = \$13.01$
$\ \ \ R\ \ \ \ - MD\ PR = MD\$$

$\dfrac{\$13.01}{\$35.00} = 37.171428\%$

Markdown \$ = \$13.01
Markdown % = 37.2%

14. $\dfrac{MD\ \$}{R} = MD\ \%$

$\dfrac{x}{\$25.00} = 25.0\% = \$6.25$

$25.00 - \$6.25 = \$18.75$
$\ \ \ R\ \ \ - MD\ \$ = MD\ PR$

Markdown \$ = \$13.01
Markdown PR = \$18.75

15. $\dfrac{MD\ PR}{R} = comp$

$100.0\% - 33.3\% = 66.7\%$

$\dfrac{\$31.99}{x} = 66.7\% = \$47.961019$

$47.96 - \$31.99 = \$15.97$
$\ \ \ R\ \ \ - MD\ PR = MD\ \$$

Retail = \$47.96
Markdown \$ = \$15.97

16. **Item #1**

$\dfrac{MD\ \$}{R} = MD\ \%$

$21.99 + \$25.00 = \$46.99$
$MD\ PR + MD\$\ =\ \ \ R$

$\dfrac{\$25.00}{\$46.99} = \% = 53.202809\%$

Item #2

$\dfrac{MD\ \$}{R} = MD\ \%$

$\dfrac{\$20.01}{x} = 41.0\% = \$48.804818$

$48.81 - \$20.01 = \$28.80$
$\ \ \ R\ \ \ - MD\$\ \ = MD\ PR$

Item #3

$\dfrac{MD\ \$}{R} = MD\ \%$

$\dfrac{x}{\$55.00} = 36.2\% = \$19.91$

$55.00 - \$19.91 = \$35.09$
$\ \ \ R\ \ \ - MD\$\ = MD\ PR$

Item #1: Retail = \$46.99
Markdown % = 53.2%
Item #2: Retail = \$48.81
Markdown total retail = \$28.80
Item #3: Markdown PR = \$35.09
Markdown \$ = \$19.91

17. See price change form on p. 311.

18. Plan

$$\frac{MD \,\$}{R} = MD \,\%$$

$$\frac{x}{\$150,000.00} = 16.0\% = \$24,000.00 \text{ PL MD } \$$$

Actual

$$\frac{MD \,\$}{R} = MD \,\%$$

$$\frac{\$20,000.00}{\$150,000.00} = x\% = 13.333\%$$

Actual MD% = 13.3%
Yes, she will make her plan.

19. Plan

$$\frac{MD \,\$}{R} = MD \,\%$$

$$\frac{x}{\$1,365,000.00} = 15\% = \$204,750.00$$

Actual

$$\frac{MD \,\$}{R} = MD \,\%$$

$$\frac{\$85,000.00}{\$1,365,000.00} = x\% = 6.2271\%$$

$ diff. = $119,750.00 less
% diff. = 8.8% less

20. See price change form on p. 312.

21. $\dfrac{Disc \,\$}{R} = Disc \,\%$

$$\frac{x}{\$162.00} = 25.5\% = \$41.31$$

$$\begin{array}{l} \$162.00 - \$41.31 = \$120.69 \\ \quad R \quad - Disc \,\$ = Disc \, PR \end{array}$$

Disc PR = $120.69

22. Skirt

$$\frac{Disc \, PR}{R} = comp \,\%$$

$$100.0\% - 20.0\% = 80.0\% \text{ comp}$$

$$\frac{\$24.00}{x} = 80.0\% = \$30.00$$

Sweater

$$\frac{Disc \, PR}{R} = comp \,\%$$

$$\frac{\$16.50}{x} = 80.0\% = \$20.625$$

Shoes

$$\frac{Disc \, PR}{R} = comp \,\%$$

$$\frac{\$19.99}{x} = 80.0\% = \$24.9875$$

Skirt = $30.00
Sweater = $20.63
Shoes = $24.99

23. $\dfrac{Disc \,\$}{R} = Disc \,\%$

$$\frac{\$17.00}{x} = 12.0\% = \$141.66666$$

$$\begin{array}{l} \$141.67 - \$16.50 = \$125.67 \\ \quad R \quad - Disc \,\$ = Disc \, PR \end{array}$$

Retail = $141.67

24. Dress

$$\frac{\text{Disc PR}}{R} = \text{comp }\%$$

$$100\% - 32.5\% = 67.5\%$$

$$\frac{\$62.00}{x} = 67.5\% = \$91.851851$$

Shoes

$$\frac{\text{Disc }\$}{R} = \text{Disc }\%$$

$$\frac{\$16.00}{x} = 32.5\% = \$49.230769$$

Coat

$$\frac{\text{Disc }\$}{R} = \text{Disc }\%$$

$$\frac{x}{\$158.00} = 32.5\% = \$51.35$$

$$\$158.00 - \$51.35 = \$106.35$$
$$\quad R \quad - \text{Disc }\$ = \text{Disc PR}$$

	Tot Disc $	Tot Retail	Tot Disc PR
Dress	$29.85	$ 91.85	$ 62.00
Shoes	$16.00	$ 49.23	$ 33.23
Coat	$ 51.35	$158.00	$106.65
	$97.20	$299.08	$201.88

Dress: **Retail= $91.85**
                  Disc $ = $29.85
Shoes: **Retail = $49.23**
                  Disc PR = 33.23
Coat: **Disc $ = $51.35**
                  Disc PR = $106.35
Total Disc $ = $97.20
Total Retail = $299.08
Total Disc PR = $201.88

25. BOM + PUR = TGH

TGH − TRR = EOM

$$\$200.0 + \$600.0 = \$800.0 \text{ TGH}$$

$$\$50.0 + \$50.0 + \$80.0 + \$5.0 = \$635.0 \text{ TRR}$$

$$\$800.0 - \$635.0 = \$165.0$$

EOM = $165.0

26. BOM + PUR = TGH

TGH − TRR = EOM

$$\$80.0 + \$250.0 = \$330.0$$

$$\$175.0 + \$25.0 + \$10.0 = \$210.0$$

$$\$330.0 - \$210.0 = \$120.0$$

EOM = $120.0

27. Actual

BOM + PUR = TGH

TGH − TRR = EOM

Phys − Book = $ Over/Short

$$\frac{\$ \text{ Over/Short}}{\text{Sales}} = \%$$

Plan − Act = Diff

$$\$100.0 + \$150.0 = \$250.0$$

$$\$250.0 - \$250.0 = 0$$
$$\text{TGH} - \text{TRR} = \text{EOM}$$

Plan

$$\frac{x}{\$200.00} = .5\% = 10$$

EOM = 0
$ Over/Short = 0
% Over/Short = 0
$ Diff vs. Plan = $1.0 less
% Diff vs. Plan = .5% less

28. BOM + PUR + AMU + Trans = TGH

    TGH – TRR = EOM

    Phys – Book = $ Over/Short

    $\dfrac{\$ \text{ Over/Short}}{\text{Sales}} = \%$

    Plan – Act = Diff

    Actual

    $50.0 +$ 550.0 +$ 10.0 + $50.0 = $660.0

    $5.0 + $35.0 +$ 5.0 + $500.0 +$ 50.0 = $595.0

    $660.0 – $595.0 = $65.0 (EOM)

    $\dfrac{\$35.0}{\$500.0} = x\% = 7.0\%$

    Plan

    $\dfrac{x}{\$500.0} = 1.0\% = \$5.0$

    1% – 7% = <6.0%>

    $5.0 – $35.0 = <$30.0>

    EOM = $65.0
    $ Short = $35.0
    % Short = 7.0%
    $ Diff = $30.0 more
    % Diff= 6.0% more

29. Sales – COGS + Cash Disc = GM

    GM – Op Exp + OP

    $\dfrac{\text{Profit factor}}{\text{Sales}} = \%$

    $\dfrac{x}{\$600.0} = 43.2\% = \$259.2$

    $\dfrac{\$361.5}{\$600.0} = x\% = 60.25\%$

    $\dfrac{x}{\$60.00} = 25.8\% = \$154.8$

$\dfrac{\$206.7}{\$ 600.0} = x\% = 34.45\%$

	$	%
Sales	$600.0	100.0%
COGS	$259.2	43.2%
CD	$ 20.7	8.0% of cost
GM	$361.5	60.3%
Op Exp	$154.8	25.8%
Op Profit	$206.7	34.5%

30. Sales – COGS + CD = GM

    GM – Op Exp = Op Profit

    $\dfrac{\text{Profit factor}}{\text{Sales}} = \%$

    $\dfrac{\$258.0}{x} = 40.2\% = \$641.79104$

    $641.8 – $258.0 + $18.0 = $401.8

    $\dfrac{\$401.8}{\$631.8} = x\% = 62.60517\%$

    $\dfrac{x}{\$641.8} = 31.8\% = \$204.0924$

    $\dfrac{\$197.7}{\$641.8} = x\% = 30.80398\%$

	$	%
Sales	$641.8	100.0%
COGS	$258.0	40.2%
CD	$ 18.0	7.0% of cost
GM	$401.8	62.6%
OE	$204.1	31.8%
OP	$197.7	30.8%

31. GM – Op Exp = P/L

    $81.3 – $85.0 = <$3.7>

    Op Loss = <$3.7>

32. $\dfrac{\$\,P/L}{Sales} = \%$

$\dfrac{\$51.0}{x} = 9.8\% = \$520.40816$

Net sales = \$520.4

33. GM − Op exp = P/L

$\$49.8 - x = <3.0>$

Op exp = \$52.8

34. NS − COGS + CD = GM − OE = OP

Gr Sales − Cost Ret = NS

\$300.0	Gross sales
− 18.0	Cust returns
\$282.0	Net sales

NS	\$ 282.0
COGS	\$ 114.6
CD	\$ 8.0
GM	\$ 174.5
CP	\$ 108.7
P/L	\$ 65.8

$\dfrac{x}{\$282.0} = \% = 38.6\% = \$108.7$

$\dfrac{\$\,114.6}{\$\,282.0} = x\% = 40.63829\%$

$\dfrac{\$\,65.8}{\$282.0} = 23.3\%$

$\dfrac{\$\,8.0}{\$114.6} = x\% = 6.9808\%$

$\dfrac{\$174.5}{\$\,282.0} = 61.87943\%$

	\$	%
Sales	**\$ 282.0**	**100.0%**
COGS	**\$ 114.6**	**40.6%**
CD	**\$ 8.0**	
GM	**\$ 174.5**	**61.9%**
Op Exp	**\$ 108.7**	**38.6%**
Op Profit	**\$ 65.8**	**23.3%**

35. NS − COGS + CD = GM − OE = P/L

$\dfrac{Profit\ factor}{Sales} = \%$

$\dfrac{\$235.0}{\$500.0} = x\% = 47.0\%$

$\$500.0 - \$235.0 + \$6.0 = \$271.0$

$\dfrac{\$271.0}{\$500.0} = \% = 54.2\%$

$\$271.0 - \$180.0 = \$91.0$

$\dfrac{\$91.0}{\$500.0} = x\% = 18.2\%$

	\$	%
Sales	**\$ 500.0**	**100.0%**
COGS	**\$ 235.0**	**47.0%**
CD	**\$ 6.0**	
GM	**\$ 271.0**	**54.2%**
Op Exp	**\$ 180.0**	**36.0%**
Op Profit	**\$ 91.0**	**18.2%**

36. Gr Sales − CR = NS

NS − COGS + CD = GM

GM − Op Exp = P/L

$\dfrac{Profit\ factor}{NS} = \%$

$\$500.0 - \$50.0 = \$450.0\ NS$

$\$450.0 - \$262.0 + 0 = \$188.0\ GM$

$\$188.0 - \$185.0 = \$3.0\ P/L$

$\dfrac{\$450.0}{\$450.0} = x\% = 100.0\%\ NS$

$\dfrac{\$262.0}{\$450.0} = \% = 58.2\%\ COGS$

$\dfrac{\$238.0}{\$450.0} = \% = 41.8\%\ GM$

$\dfrac{\$185.0}{\$450.0} = \% = 37.0\%\ Exp$

$$\frac{\$3.0}{\$450.0} = \% = .7\% \text{ Profit}$$

	$	%
NS	$ 450.0	100.0%
COGS	$ 262.0	58.2%
CD	$ 0	0 %
GM	$ 188.0	41.8%
Exp	$ 185.0	37.0%
Profit	$ 3.0	.7%

PURCHASE ORDER

STORE NAME: _____

DEPT: _____

ORDER DATE: _____

DO NOT SHIP BEFORE: _____

CANCEL IF NOT RECD: _____

VENDOR: _____

ADDRESS: _____

FREIGHT ALLOWANCE: _____

FOB PT: _____

SHIP VIA: _____

TERMS: _____ % EOM

NO: _____

CLASS	DESCRIPTION	STYLE	SIZE	COLOR	TOTAL UNITS	COST EA	COST TOT	RET EA	RET TOT	MU%	MU$
	Culottes	5106			28	$12.00	$336.00	$30.00	$840.00	60.0%	
	Sweaters	6106			28	$25.00	$700.00	$55.00	$1,540.00	54.6%	
	T-shirts	8106			59	$9.00	$531.00	$18.52	$1,092.68	51.4%	
	Slacks	9106			36	$10.00	$360.00	$26.00	$936.00	61.5%	
	Shorts	9206			28	$6.66	$186.48	$15.00	$420.00	55.6%	
	Jackets	2106			28	$34.31	$960.68	$73.31	$2,052.68	53.2%	
		TOTALS			207		$3,074.16		$6,881.36	55.3%	

BUYER'S SIGNATURE: _____

PURCHASE ORDER   NO: _____

STORE NAME: _____

DEPT: _____   VENDOR: _____   FREIGHT ALLOWANCE: _____
ORDER DATE: _____   ADDRESS: _____   FOB PT: _____
DO NOT SHIP BEFORE: _____   SHIP VIA: _____
CANCEL IF NOT RECD: _____   TERMS: _____ % EOM

CLASS	DESCRIPTION	STYLE	SIZE	COLOR	TOTAL UNITS	COST EA	COST TOT	RET EA	RET TOT	MU%	MU$
	Sandals	0016		white	168	$15.00	$2,520.00	$31.12	$5,228.16	51.8%	
	Sandals	0017		beige	197	$17.36.	$3,419.92	$34.86	$6,869.42	50.2%	
	Sandals	0018		tan	216	$15.15	$3,272.40	$30.99	$6,693.84	51.1%	
		TOTALS			581		$9,212.32		$18,789.42	51.0%	

BUYER'S SIGNATURE: _____

	Quantity	Unit Cost	Cost Ext.	Unit Retail	Retail Ext.	Markup %
Total Needed			$367.2		$ 80.0	(45.9%) 54.1%
Already Bought			$300.0		$612.24489	(49.0%) 51.0%
Balance-to-Buy			$ 67.2		$187.75511	64.2%

	Quantity	Unit Cost	Cost Ext.	Unit Retail	Retail Ext.	Markup %
Total Needed	2,000		$10,726.24	$10.99	$21,980.00	(48.8%) 51.2%
Already Bought	1,250		$ 7,125.00	$10.99	$13,737.50	48.1%
Balance-to-Buy	750	$4.80	$ 3,601.24	$10.99	$ 8,242.50	56.3%

	Quantity	Unit Cost	Cost Ext.	Unit Retail	Retail Ext.	Markup %
Total Needed			$696.0		$ 1,500.0	(46.4%) 53.6%
Already Bought			$535.0		$ 1,133.4745	(47.3%) 52.8%
Balance-to-Buy			$161.0		$ 366.5255	56.1%

	Quantity	Unit Cost	Cost Ext.	Unit Retail	Retail Ext.	Markup %
Total Needed	600		$$357.0		$750.0	(47.6%) 52.4%
Already Bought	400		$ 300.0		$625.0	(48.0%) 52.0%
Balance-to-Buy	200	$285.00	$ 57.0	$625.00	$125.0	54.4%

PRICE CHANGE

NO.: _____

DATE: _____

STORE: _____

DEPT.: _____

Indicate type of price change with an X.
Use separate sheet for each type of change.

X	Markdown
---	Markdown Cancellation
---	Markup
---	Markup Cancellation

CLASS	MFG	DESCRIPTION	UNITS	OLD RET	NEW RET	DIFFERENCE	EXTENSION	MD%
			62	$16.00	$11.01	$4.99	$309.38	31.2%
			38	$39.99	$25.99	$14.00	$532.00	
			51	$37.46	$14.46	$23.00	$1,173.00	61.4%
						TOTAL	$2,014.38	45.6%

SIGNATURE: _____

PRICE CHANGE

NO.: _____

DATE: _____

STORE: _____

DEPT: _____

Indicate type of price change with an X.
Use separate sheet for each type of change.

X	Markdown
	Markdown Cancellation
	Markup
	Markup Cancellation

CLASS	MFG	DESCRIPTION	UNITS	OLD RET	NEW RET	DIFFERENCE	EXTENSION	MD%
		Item #1	162	$46.99	$21.99	$25.00	$4,050.00	
		Item #2	53	$48.81	$28.80	$20.01	$1,060.53	
		Item #3	201	$55.00	$35.09	$19.91	$4,001.91	
					TOTAL	$9,112.44	42.9%

SIGNATURE: _____

ABOUT THE AUTHORS

Andrea L. Weeks is currently a merchandise/marketing coordinator and marketing instructor at The Fashion Institute of Design and Merchandising in Los Angeles, California. After receiving her bachelor of arts degree from the University of California at Irvine, she was hired by Bullock's Department Stores as a management trainee. After six years of being promoted to various levels of management positions, she was appointed buyer for the men's furnishings department. In 1981, she left retailing to join the marketing faculty at The Fashion Institute of Design and Merchandising. In her current position, she is involved in developing the marketing, mathematics, and computer curricula.

Madelyn C. Perenchio received her college education at Bradley University in Illinois. She was recruited as a management trainee for Charles A. Stevens Specialty Store. After rising to the position of buyer, she then joined Robinson's management team. From there, she went to Diamonds as a buyer of fashion accessories. Broadway Department Stores then recruited her as an assistant store manager in charge of merchandising where she rose to become a regional marketing coordinator in cosmetics. In 1982, Madelyn was recruited by The Fashion Institute of Design and Merchandising to teach merchandising and management. She is currently a full-time instructor at Los Angeles City College. Additional current industry experience includes: vice-president of marketing, Clay Images by Justin; vice-president of marketing at Studio House Productions; and president/owner of Madelyn Perenchio and Associates Marketing Consultants.

Veronica "Roni" J. Miller received her bachelor of science degree in business administration from California State University, Haywood. She then received her masters of business administration at California State University, Northridge. Upon graduation, she was recruited by Broadway Department Stores as a management trainee. She served as a buyer for the men's better sportswear and sport tailored clothing for five years. She is currently a marketing instructor at The Fashion Institute of Design and Merchandising, Pierce College, Los Angeles City College, and Golden Gate University. In addition to her duties as an instructor, she also owns a marketing consultation firm—RJM & Associates.

Dorothy A. Metcalfe is currently the chairperson of the Merchandise Marketing Department at the Fashion Institute of Design and Merchandising. She received her baccalaureate degree from the University of California in Los Angeles. She was recruited by the Broadway Department Stores as a Management trainee and rose to the position of buyer in the accessories department. She left the Broadway to join the faculty at the Fashion Institute, rising to her current position, which involves the planning and direction of the curriculum. Additional activities include: member of the board of directors for the Academy of Visual Arts; state advisor for California for Delta Epsilon Chi, and owner and president of D.A.M. & Associates, a retail consulting firm.

INDEX

A

Actual, 178
Additional markup, 177, 178
Advanced dating, 101
Advertising, 53, 55, 227
Averages, 109
Average markup, 111
Averaging of markups, 109

B

Balance–to–buy, 110, 111
Beginning–of–month (BOM), 208, 223
Book or statistical ending inventory (EOM), 207, 208
Book or statistical inventory, 207, 208
Business image, 55

C

Capital for reinvestment, 227, 243
Cash discount, 55, 90, 99, 100, 227, 243
Causes of markdowns, 178
Claims, 208
Classification, 54
Clearance sale, 178
Closing inventory procedures, 247, 278
Concepts of averaging, 111
Cost of goods, 226
Cost of merchandise, 29, 31
Cost of merchandise sold, 226
Cost or retail inventory, 207
Cumulative markup percent, 247, 278
Cumulative quantity discount, 91
Customer acceptance, 29, 54
Customer returns and allowances, 208, 209, 210, 212

D

Dating, 90
Delivery, 53, 54
Difference, 178
Different appeal/different markup, 110, 111
Different market/different markup, 109, 111
Different purpose/different markup, 110, 111
Discount dollars, 178
Discount price, 178
Dividends, 227, 243
Dollar difference, 14, 27

E

Employee discount, 29, 30, 178
Employee discount percent, 178
End–of–month (EOM), 91, 216, 218, 219, 221
Expenses, 226, 227, 243
Extension, 55

F

Fall quarter, 175
Final Review, 279
Free–on–board (FOB), 91
Four–five–four fiscal calendar, 175
Freight, 55, 247, 278
Freight terms, 54, 90, 91

G

Goals, 111
Gross margin, 226, 227, 240
Gross profit, 247, 278
Gross sales, 208, 227, 240
Grouping of purchases, 55

H

Holiday quarter, 175

I

Initial markup, 55
International buying, 31
Inventory, 205-223
    accurate assessment, 206
    basic closing rules, 214, 215
    book (See Book inventory)
    cost, 207
    insurance, 206
    levels, 206
    overage, 208, 209
    physical, 207, 209
    profit statement, 207
    reconciliation, 208
    shortage, 208, 209
    sold, 226
    sufficient stock levels, 206
    taxes, 206
    total goods handled, 208, 209
    total retail reductions, 207, 208, 209
Invoice, 91

J

Jobber, 91

L

Lead time, 208
Line, 55

M

Markdown, 29, 178
Markdowns, 29, 177
Markdown cancellations (MDC), 178
Markdown dollars, 178

Markdown price, 178
Market, 47
Markup cancellations (MUC), 177, 178
Markup dollars, 31, 32
Markup percent, 31, 32
Measurement of improvement, 13
Measurement of progress, 13
Merchandise marketing, 30

N

Negotiation, 89, 91, 107
Net invoice charges, 91
Net sales, 225, 227, 243
New amount, 14, 27
Non-cumulative quantity discount, 91

O

Open–to–buy (OTB), 111
Operating statement, 225, 227, 243
Original amount, 14, 27
Overage or shortage, 208, 209
Overbuying, 178
Overhead (expenses), 226

P

Percentage, 13, 14, 27
Percentage increase/decrease, 13
Physical inventory, 207, 208, 209
Preparation of profit statement, 207, 209
Price change form, 176
Profit, 227, 243
Profit percent, 227, 243
Purchase order, 54, 55
Purchases, 111, 247

Q

Quantity discount, 89, 91

R

Reasons of markdowns, 179
Receipts, 111
Receipt of goods, 91
Reconciliation, 208
Retail, 32, 179
Retail reductions, 29
Retail sales, 179
Returns and allowances, 227, 243
ROG, 91, 107
Rounding, 1
Rounding methods, 1, 2, 6

S

Salaries, 227, 243
Seasonal plan, 109
Shortage, 30, 208, 209
Shrinkage reserve, 209, 247
Simple profit or loss, 207, 209
Special purchase, 179
Spring quarter, 175, 179
Sufficient stock levels, 206
Suggested list price, 91
Summer quarter, 175, 179

T

Taxes and insurance required, 206
Terms of the sale, 89, 91
Total cost, 111
Total goods handled, 208
Total needed, 110, 111
Total retail, 111
Total retail reductions, 207, 208
Trade discount, 90, 91
Transfer, 209
Transfers in, 209
Transfers out, 209
Truncating method, 2

V

Visual impact, 55

W

Workroom, 246, 247, 278

WE VALUE YOUR OPINION—PLEASE SHARE IT WITH US

Merrill Publishing and our authors are most interested in your reactions to this textbook. Did it serve you well in the course? If it did, what aspects of the text were most helpful? If not, what didn't you like about it? Your comments will help us to write and develop better textbooks. We value your opinions and thank you for your help.

Text Title _____ Edition _____

Author(s) _____

Your Name (optional) _____

Address _____

City _____ State _____ Zip _____

School _____

Course Title _____

Instructor's Name _____

Your Major _____

Your Class Rank _____ Freshman _____ Sophomore _____ Junior _____ Senior

_____ Graduate Student

Were you required to take this course? _____ Required _____ Elective

Length of Course? _____ Quarter _____ Semester

1. Overall, how does this text compare to other texts you've used?

_____ Superior _____ Better Than Most _____ Average _____ Poor

2. Please rate the text in the following areas:

	Superior	Better Than Most	Average	Poor
Author's Writing Style	_____	_____	_____	_____
Readability	_____	_____	_____	_____
Organization	_____	_____	_____	_____
Accuracy	_____	_____	_____	_____
Layout and Design	_____	_____	_____	_____
Illustrations/Photos/Tables	_____	_____	_____	_____
Examples	_____	_____	_____	_____
Problems/Exercises	_____	_____	_____	_____
Topic Selection	_____	_____	_____	_____
Currentness of Coverage	_____	_____	_____	_____
Explanation of Difficult Concepts	_____	_____	_____	_____
Match-up with Course Coverage	_____	_____	_____	_____
Applications to Real Life	_____	_____	_____	_____

3. Circle those chapters you especially liked:

   1   2   3   4   5   6   7   8   9   10   11   12   13   14   15   16   17   18   19   20

   What was your favorite chapter? _____
   Comments:

4. Circle those chapters you liked least:

   1   2   3   4   5   6   7   8   9   10   11   12   13   14   15   16   17   18   19   20

   What was your least favorite chapter? _____
   Comments:

5. List any chapters your instructor did not assign. _____

6. What topics did your instructor discuss that were not covered in the text?_____

   _____

7. Were you required to buy this book? _____ Yes _____ No

   Did you buy this book new or used? _____ New _____ Used

   If used, how much did you pay? _____

   Do you plan to keep or sell this book? _____ Keep _____ Sell

   If you plan to sell the book, how much do you expect to receive? _____

   Should the instructor continue to assign this book? _____ Yes _____ No

8. Please list any other learning materials you purchased to help you in this course (e.g., study guide, lab manual).

   _____

9. What did you like most about this text? _____

   _____

10. What did you like least about this text? _____

   _____

11. General comments:

   May we quote you in our advertising? _____ Yes _____ No

   Please mail to: Boyd Lane
                      College Division, Research Department
                      Box 508
                      1300 Alum Creek Drive
                      Columbus, Ohio 43216

   Thank you!